Public Asset Management Companies

A WORLD BANK STUDY

Public Asset Management Companies

A Toolkit

Caroline Cerruti and Ruth Neyens

WORLD BANK GROUP

Contents

Boxes

Figures

Tables

Executive Summary

Distressed assets and nonperforming loans (NPLs) are part of life for financial institutions. In normal times, financial institutions should be able to manage such assets: they know their clients and their capacity to repay, thus they are best prepared to restructure and collect on the NPLs. However, a more direct intervention may be warranted when (i) the level of nonperforming assets throughout the system is high, and threatens the stability of the financial system; (ii) the banks are unwilling or unable to recognize their losses due to thin capital positions or lack the necessary skills to restructure the loans; and/or (iii) the legislative framework for debt enforcement is weak or unable to accommodate a large number of cases.

Some countries affected by banking crises and high levels of NPLs have established distressed-asset management companies (AMCs). An AMC is a public, private, or joint entity that manages nonperforming assets removed from the financial system with the goal of maximizing the recovery value of these assets. It can be established either as an entity tasked with resolving failed financial institutions and liquidating their assets, or as an entity that purchases assets from open banks.

An AMC may benefit a financial system in several ways. First, it forces banks to recognize their losses. Although this may result in fiscal costs if the banks need

AMCs Studied

AMC	Country
Resolution Trust Corporation (RTC)	United States
Securum	Sweden
Korea Asset Management Corporation (KAMCO)	Republic of Korea
Indonesian Bank Restructuring Agency (IBRA)	Indonesia
Danaharta	Malaysia
Savings Deposit Insurance Fund (SDIF)	Turkey
National Asset Management Agency (NAMA)	Ireland
Asset Management Corporation of Nigeria (AMCON)	Nigeria
Sociedad de Gestión de Activos Procedentes de la Reestructuración Bancaria (SAREB)	Spain

public assistance to recapitalize, it is a necessary action to restore confidence in the system. Second, the use of cash and/or a coupon-paying government-guaranteed security to purchase nonperforming assets from open banks may improve asset quality and provide the financial institutions with badly needed income. Also, these securities may provide liquidity if they can be used as collateral for borrowings from the central bank. Third, the financial system is strengthened by restructuring weak but viable banks and their borrowers, and removing those that are not viable. Additional benefits cited for the use of an AMC include economies of scale and enhanced bargaining power owing to their size and specialization, and enabling banks to focus on new lending while allowing the AMC to concentrate on the recovery of impaired assets. Thus AMCs can be crucial for price discovery and bridging the pricing gap in situations where no market exists or the market is extremely illiquid.

However, to ensure the success of the AMC, certain preconditions should be in place. The preconditions relate to (i) a commitment to comprehensive reforms, (ii) a systemic problem and public funds at risk, (iii) a solid diagnostic and critical mass of impaired assets, (iv) a tradition of institutional independence and public accountability, and (v) a robust legal framework for bank resolution, debt recovery, and creditors' rights.

The analysis of nine case studies of AMCs in this toolkit shows that AMCs have a mixed track record. AMCs are costly to establish and to operate; therefore their costs and benefits should be assessed carefully before they are established. Most of the AMCs created in the wake of the global financial crisis have been structured as entities purchasing assets from open banks. More recently, in Europe, the private sector has participated in ownership of the AMC to avoid consolidation in the national accounts. This has raised issues regarding transfer price, voluntary versus mandatory participation of financial institutions, and eligibility of assets for purchase. For the purposes of this paper, AMCs have been considered to be successful when they managed to repay all their liabilities and some of their initial equity. Some AMCs that did not have high face-value returns managed to achieve other results (such as the creation of a vibrant distressed-asset market, or the recovery of misused liquidity support from the shareholders of the failed banks).

The analysis of case studies over 1990–2015 provided the following insights (table 0.1 for selected good practices and table 3.2 for key characteristics of the AMCs studied):

- AMCs have been established either to resolve insolvent financial institutions and their assets, or to purchase assets from open banks; one, Malaysia's Dana-harta, performed both functions.
- AMCs benefit from a high level of consensus and political will, particularly with respect to a willingness to crystallize, or recognize, the true level of losses within the banking system.

- When AMCs have purchased assets from open banks, defining the transfer price was the most difficult design issue. Participation from financial institutions was either made mandatory or associated with strong regulatory incentives to participate.
- Most successful AMCs have had a narrow mandate (such as resolving NPLs) with clearly defined goals, a sunset clause, and a commercial focus, including governance, transparency, and disclosure requirements.
- AMCs do not have to be a new institution; sometimes an existing institution, such as a deposit insurance agency, can be retooled to perform the asset management function.
- Although some AMCs needed special powers when the legal and regulatory framework for debt enforcement was deficient, all benefited from complementary programs to strengthen regulation and supervision, legal and judicial reforms, and improvements in governance.

The toolkit seeks to inform policy makers on issues to consider if and when they are planning the creation of a public AMC. It does not intend to address broader bank resolution issues. It has a narrow focus on the specific tool of a public (that is, majority ownership by the government or significant government participation as in Europe) AMC established to support bank resolution, and its objective is to provide insight on the design and operational issues surrounding the creation of such AMCs. The paper is structured as follows: Part I summarizes the findings on the preconditions, the design, and the operationalization of public AMCs. Part II provides case studies on three generations of AMCs, whose lessons are embedded in Part I. The case studies cover emerging and developed markets, and have been selected based on the lessons they offer.

Figure 0.1 Key Design Issues to Enhance AMC Performance

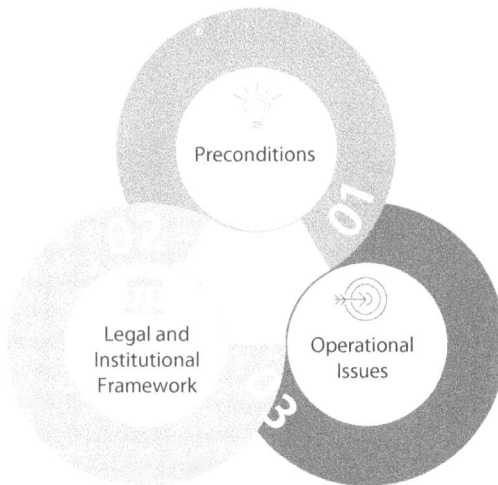

Source: World Bank.

Table 0.1 Good Practices for AMCs

Issue	Practice	Examples

Preconditions	Successful AMCs require basic preconditions:
	• Strong consensus and political will with respect to the approach, and willingness to recognize losses
	• Comprehensive and coordinated reform program to strengthen financial sector regulation and supervision, risk management and workout practices within the banks, corporate restructuring, and legal and regulatory reforms to remove impediments to restructuring
	• Solid diagnostic and critical mass of impaired assets
	
	• Strong tradition of institutional independence and public accountability
	• Robust legal framework for bank resolution, debt recovery, and creditors' rights
		• The RTC, KAMCO, NAMA: political consensus
		  Securum: willingness to recognize losses
		• Securum and Danaharta: part of a comprehensive solution to restore financial stability
		  Ireland: strengthened financial supervision and reformed insolvency
		• SAREB: created after a comprehensive evaluation of the assets of the banking system
		  Danaharta: determined the threshold of eligible loans so as to remove a significant portion of NPLs in the banking system (70 percent)
		• Sweden: history of responsible ownership of state-owned enterprises.
		• RTC: benefited from FDIC bank resolution methodology, robust framework for debt recovery
		  Korea: adopted policies and legal reforms to facilitate corporate restructuring, created KAMCO

Legal and institutional framework	• Clearly focused and narrow mandate with necessary powers to accomplish tasks
	• Use of special powers should be limited both in time and scope, and subject to enhanced oversight to limit abuse
	• Strong commercial focus reflected in majority of board membership from private sector, chief executive officer (CEO) with demonstrated private sector experience in asset management, and staff with appropriate market-based skills
	• Strong levels of governance, with frequent reporting including annual financial statements
	• Adequate funding provided up front to cover operating expenses until proceeds of asset sales received
		• Securum, Danaharta
		  Counter-example: IBRA, whose mandate was overly broad
		• Danaharta: oversight committee for its use of special powers
		• Danaharta (board members from private sector and international experts); also NAMA and SAREB
		  The SDIF: institutional-strengthening program
		• Danaharta, the SDIF, KAMCO, NAMA, SAREB: frequent public reporting
		• Securum
		  Counter-example: The RTC, where funding delays hampered recovery efforts

table continues next page

Table 0.1 Good Practices for AMCs (continued)

Issue	Practice	Examples
	• Transfer price based on market value established through a transparent, market-based, due diligence process conducted with the assistance of an independent third party experienced in valuation • Ensure adequate safeguard mechanisms through enhanced transparency and reporting standards, use of fixed sunset date, and/or limited period to acquire assets and amount of bonds it can issue	• NAMA and SAREB: made use of independent third-party experts for valuation, in accordance with their transparent methodology • SAREB: limit on the bonds it can issue The RTC, IBRA, and SAREB: sunset clause KAMCO: limited period for asset purchase
Operational issues	• Consider use of private contractors whenever possible, with appropriate oversight from the AMC • Develop strategic plan as well as detailed business plans, with frequent review and corrective action plans when necessary	• RTC and Danaharta: outsourced extensively Counter-example: IBRA, where the outsourcing of restructuring to banks failed • NAMA: various business plans, accessible online
	• Ensure strong internal controls and transparency to reduce the possible misuse of funds • Move rapidly toward asset disposition • Document the history of the AMC in detail and publish on permanent website	• RTC: beefed up internal controls after initial failure • Securum, RTC, KAMCO, and Danaharta: moved rapidly to dispose assets KAMCO: created a market for distressed assets using international expertise through joint ventures • The RTC, KAMCO, Danaharta, IBRA, and the SDIF: documented their experience in detail

Note: These are selected examples drawn from the report. They are not exhaustive. The case studies provide additional examples. AMC = asset management company; CEO = chief executive officer; FDIC = Federal Deposit Insurance Corporation; IBRA = Indonesian Bank Restructuring Agency (Indonesia); KAMCO = Korea Asset Management Corporation (Korea); NAMA = National Asset Management Agency (Ireland); NPL = nonperforming loan; RTC = Resolution Trust Corporation (United States); SAREB = Sociedad de Gestión de Activos Procedentes de la Reestructuración Bancaria (Spain); SDIF = Savings Deposit Insurance Fund (Turkey).

Glossary of Technical Terms

Asset management company (AMC) Public, private, or joint entity that manages nonperforming assets removed from the financial system with the goal of maximizing the recovery value of these assets.

Asset quality review (AQR) Comprehensive review or evaluation of a financial institution's assets to assess the adequacy of asset and collateral valuations and related provisions.

Connected, insider, or related-party loans Loans made to bank shareholders, directors, managers, or other key employees and their closely related family members, business ventures, or friends.

Corporate restructuring Process of classifying financially distressed firms as either viable or nonviable. The financial structure of viable firms is then modified to create sustainable financial and operational performance, while nonviable firms are liquidated. Financial restructuring generally takes the form of extending maturities, lowering interest rates, modifying repayment schedules, or injecting additional equity. Operational restructuring, which must be led by management or owners, includes management changes, reductions in staff or wages, and asset sales.

Eligible institution Bank or other financial institutions that may transfer or sell nonperforming assets to an AMC.

Key performance indicators Set of quantifiable measures used to monitor an AMC's performance in terms of meeting its strategic and operational goals.

Long-term economic value Value that an asset can reasonably be expected to attain in a stable financial system when the crisis conditions prevailing at the time of the valuation are ameliorated and in which the future price or yield of the asset is consistent with reasonable expectations, having regard to the long-term historical average.[1]

Market value Estimated amount for which an asset or liability should exchange on the valuation date between a willing buyer and a willing seller in an arm's

---

1. Opinion of the ECB of August 31, 2009 on the establishment of the National Asset Management Agency, Section 1.4, p. 3, https://www.nama.ie/fileadmin/user_upload/ECB_opinion_re_NAMA31 AUGUST2009.pdf.

length transaction, after proper marketing and where the parties have each acted knowledgeably, prudently, and without compulsion.[2]

Negative equity (financial institution) Amount by which the liabilities of a financial institution exceed its assets so that the equity is wiped out and may reach a negative value.

Nonperforming loans (NPLs) Loans on which principal or interest payments are more than 90 days in arrears.

Power of sale Mortgage lender's right to sell a property upon loan default without a judicial proceeding. This power is generally contained in the mortgage document. In jurisdictions that require judicial foreclosure, the power of sale is frequently granted to an AMC to provide a timely and cost-effective recovery method. Sale proceeds in excess of the legal obligation (including costs as defined by the loan documents) must be returned to the owner.

Sale by private treaty Sale of property between two parties that agree among themselves to the terms of the sale.

Special powers Extrajudicial powers granted to an AMC to facilitate the recovery process. Common examples include the right to exercise the power of sale, the ability to transfer ownership of loans without the borrower's consent, and the ability to appoint a special administrator. The powers require strong governance to ensure that they are not abused and should be granted for a limited period of time.

Structured financial products Investments uniquely designed to provide investors with risk-return, tax, and diversification characteristics that are not generally available from traditional investments.

Termination or sunset date Specific date on which an AMC is to terminate its existence.

Transfer price Price at which NPLs are purchased by an AMC. This price should closely approximate the market value of the assets purchased.

Vesting order Order transferring legal ownership (including the right to seek relief under loan documents or in court if payment is not received) of NPLs from a bank to an AMC. This method does not require the consent of the borrower.

---

2. International Valuation Standards Council, http://www.ivsc.org/standards/glossary#letter_m.

Abbreviations

ABS	asset-backed security
AIB	Allied Irish Bank
AMC	asset management company
AMCON	Asset Management Corporation of Nigeria
AQR	asset quality review
BI	Bank Indonesia
BNM	Bank Negara Malaysia
BOI	Bank of Ireland
BOK	Bank of Korea
BoS	Bank of Spain
BRSA	Banking Supervisory Agency of Turkey
CAR	capital adequacy ratio
CBN	Central Bank of Nigeria
CBT	Central Bank of Turkey
CDRC	Corporate Debt Restructuring Committee
CEO	chief executive officer
CNMV	Securities and Exchange Commission of Spain
CPA	certified public accountant
CRA	corporate restructuring agreement
EBS	Educational Building Society (Ireland)
EBITDA	earnings before interest, taxes, depreciation, and amortization
EC	European Commission
FDIC	Federal Deposit Insurance Corporation
FIRREA	Financial Institutions Reform, Recovery, and Enforcement Act
FROB	Fondo de Reestructuración Ordenada Bancaria
FSAP	Financial Sector Assessment Program
FSC	Financial Supervisory Commission
FSLIC	Federal Savings and Loan Insurance Corporation
GDP	gross domestic product

GNP	gross national product
IBRA	Indonesian Bank Restructuring Agency (Indonesia)
IFRS	International Financial Reporting Standards
ILP	Irish Life and Permanent plc
INBS	Irish Nationwide Building Society
INSOL	International Association of Restructuring, Insolvency, and Bankruptcy Professionals
IPO	initial public offering
IRS	interest rate swap
JITF	Jakarta Initiative Task Force
KAMCO	Korea Asset Management Corporation (Korea)
KDB	Korea Development Bank
KDIC	Korea Deposit Insurance Corporation
KOB	Czech Consolidation Bank
KOR	Republic of Korea
KPI	key performance indicator
M&A	merger and acquisition
MOF	Ministry of Finance
MOFE	Ministry of Finance and Economy
MoU	memorandum of understanding
NAMA	National Asset Management Agency (Ireland)
NDIC	Nigeria Deposit Insurance Corporation
NPA	Non-performing Asset Management Fund (Korea)
NPL	nonperforming loan
RA	Revitalization Agency (Czech Republic)
RE	real estate
REFCORP	Resolution Funding Corporation (United States)
RTC	Resolution Trust Corporation (United States)
S&L	Saving and Loan Association
SAREB	Sociedad de Gestión de Activos Procedentes de la Reestructuración Bancaria (Spain)
SDIF	Savings Deposit Insurance Fund (Turkey)
SPV	special-purpose vehicle

Introduction

This toolkit is designed for policy makers and stakeholders who are considering the establishment of a publicly funded asset management company (AMC).[1] An AMC is a statutory body or corporation, usually established in times of financial sector stress, to assume the management of distressed assets and recoup a portion of the public cost of resolving the crisis.

AMCs were first used in the early 1990s in Sweden (Securum) and the United States (the RTC), and again during the Asian crisis (Danaharta in Malaysia, KAMCO in the Republic of Korea). The 2008 financial crisis marked a renewal of the use of this tool to support the resolution of financial crises (for instance, NAMA in Ireland, SAREB in Spain).

The toolkit does not address broader bank resolution issues. It has a narrow focus on the specific tool of a public AMC established to support bank resolution, and its objective is to provide insight on the design and operational issues surrounding the creation of such AMCs. Based on a review of various cases, it seeks to inform policy makers on issues to consider if and when planning to establish an AMC. Public AMCs are defined as fully or partially government-owned AMCs; in recent European cases, the private sector has participated in the ownership to avoid consolidation in the national accounts.

There is a growing body of research on the design and performance of public AMCs, particularly in the aftermath of the Asian crisis, when several of these institutions were created. This paper seeks to bring a more up to date and practical perspective through four efforts:

- An analysis of recent public AMCs established as a result of the global financial crisis
- Detailed case studies in developed and emerging markets over three generations
- A toolkit approach with questions and answers, including questions on design and operations that are critical for authorities confronted with the issue of whether to establish an AMC
- An emphasis on "how to" that is, a practical versus a principled approach.

The toolkit is structured as followed: Part I summarizes the findings on the preconditions, the design, and the operationalization of public AMCs. Part II provides case studies on three generations of AMCs, whose lessons are embedded in Part I. The case studies cover emerging and developed markets, and have been selected based on the lessons they offer.

Note

1. The authors are particularly indebted to Nagavalli Annamalai, Alfonso Garcia-Mora, Ceyla Pazarbasioglu, Antonia Menezes, Jan Nolte, and Roberto Rocha for their helpful review and comments. The case studies would not have been made possible without the contributions and thorough review of Somender Chaudhary, Michael Fuchs, Enrique Martin (SAREB), Paula Perttunen, Sergio Pinto, and Martin Whelan (NAMA). Monzerrat Garcia provided excellent editorial assistance.

Many thanks to Liudmila Uvarova for her help and drive to get this paper published. Finally, the authors are particularly grateful to the Department of International Development of the United Kingdom, whose support was instrumental in bringing this paper to fruition.

PART I

The AMC Toolkit

An asset management company (AMC) is an entity established to manage and enhance recoveries of distressed assets removed from the financial system. It can be established either as an entity tasked with resolving failed financial institutions and liquidating their assets, or as an entity that purchases assets from open banks. In the first case, the AMC does not select and purchase the distressed assets. Instead, under the banking law, it is appointed to restructure or liquidate insolvent banks, in whole or in part (usually after the protected deposits have been transferred). Thus, no financial transaction or purchase takes place and the AMCs' assets are very diverse in size and type. In the second case, the AMC purchases assets from banks that are still operating. These assets must meet certain characteristics as defined by the legislation or the AMC. A financial transaction takes place between the selling bank and the AMC, and usually the AMC issues a government-guaranteed bond to pay for the purchase. In both cases, the value of the assets must be established by a prior assessment or valuation of the assets by the supervisor, or by the AMC through a transparent, market-based, due diligence process conducted by an independent third party experienced in valuation. Figure I.1 illustrates schematically the two types of AMCs.

Figure I.1 Two Schematic Types of Public AMC

Bank resolution AMC   Asset purchasing AMC

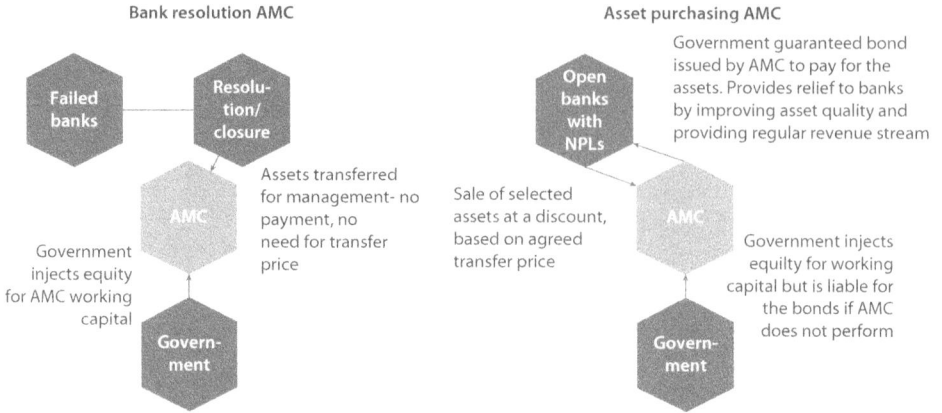

Note: In this figure, the asset-purchasing AMC reflects the most recent generation of such entities. In the 1990s, AMCs involved in asset management did not issue bonds to the banks; instead the state issued these bonds (as in the case of Eastern European countries and the Indonesian Bank Restructuring Agency, or IBRA). More recently in Europe, the trend has been to create public-private AMCs to avoid consolidation in the public accounts. AMC = asset management company; IBRA = Indonesian Bank Restructuring Agency (Indonesia).
Source: World Bank

CHAPTER 1

Why a Public AMC? Preconditions for Public AMCs

Asset management is a function, not an institution. In a context of a financial system crisis or high nonperforming loans (NPLs), establishing a publicly funded institution is not necessarily the most appropriate answer. Alternate resolution tools include establishing workout departments within the banks or establishing a separate subsidiary to handle the recovery process. In a number of countries, the AMC has been part of the crisis resolution framework either as a bank resolution entity (to restructure, sell, and liquidate failed banks), or as an entity purchasing NPLs in exchange for securities. However, the tool is successful only if certain preconditions are met and the design is carefully thought through. It is also possible that an existing institution may be retooled to implement the function of asset management. The Savings Deposit Insurance Fund (SDIF; Turkey) and the Korean Asset Management Corporation (KAMCO) provide such examples.

In normal times, banks and financial institutions should be able to manage their NPLs. They know their clients and their capacity to repay, thus they are best prepared to restructure and collect on the NPLs. However, a more direct intervention may be warranted when (i) the level of nonperforming assets throughout the system is high and threatens the stability of the financial system; (ii) the banks are unwilling to recognize their losses due to thin capital positions or lack the necessary skills and expertise to restructure the loans; or (iii) the legislative framework for debt enforcement is weak or unable to accommodate a large number of cases.

An AMC may benefit the financial system in several ways. First it forces the banks to recognize their losses. Although this may result in fiscal costs if the banks need public assistance to recapitalize, it is a necessary action that may help to restore confidence in the system. Second, the use of cash or a coupon-paying, government-guaranteed security to purchase nonperforming (nonearning assets) from open banks may improve asset quality and provide badly needed income to the financial institutions. Also, these securities may provide liquidity if they can be used as collateral for borrowings from the central bank. Third, the financial system is strengthened by restructuring weak but viable banks and their borrowers, and removing those that are not viable. In Eastern Europe in the 1990s, AMCs contributed to the privatization of the banking system. Additional benefits cited for the use of an AMC include economies of scale through reducing the fixed cost of asset resolution, increasing the efficiency of asset recovery, and allowing for more efficient packaging of assets for sale to outside specialist investors; enhanced bargaining power relative to the borrowers, particularly when loans are scattered throughout the system, collateral is pledged to multiple creditors, and the size of debtors is large relative to the size of banks; and specialization by enabling banks to focus on new lending while allowing the AMC to concentrate on the recovery of impaired assets, which can facilitate better valuation and credit discipline. These points taken together suggest that AMCs could be crucial to price discovery and bridging the pricing gap in situations where no market exists or the market is extremely illiquid (Aiyar et al. 2015).

Yet the case studies show that certain preconditions need to be in place to make the creation of an AMC worthwhile and to ensure its success. The preconditions relate to (i) a commitment to comprehensive reforms; (ii) a systemic problem and public funds at risk; (iii) a solid diagnostic and critical mass of impaired assets; (iv) a tradition of institutional independence and public accountability; and (v) a robust legal framework for bank resolution, debt recovery, and creditors' rights. AMCs are costly to establish and to operate; therefore their costs and benefits should be assessed carefully before they are created (as in the case of the National Asset Management Agency (NAMA) in Ireland, where the Bacon report examined all the options for dealing with the crisis before recommending the use of a public AMC).

If these preconditions are not met, other options should be considered, on the basis of each country's circumstances. One option that benefits the whole financial system is to improve the framework for debt enforcement so as to facilitate the enforcement of collateral (box 1.1 discusses the Latvian experience). It may, however, take considerable time to change the practices regarding insolvency or foreclosure beyond legislation, and doing so requires buy-in from multiple stakeholders. Informal, voluntary workout frameworks based on the London Approach may help but need to work in the shadow of a strong insolvency framework in order to be effective. If distressed assets are confined to a limited number of institutions, a special-purpose vehicle (SPV) could be established as a subsidiary of the bank or its holding company to work out the assets, together with an asset guarantee scheme (the solution adopted in the United Kingdom with the Royal Bank of Scotland). This assumes that the bank will have the capability to implement the workout. Another option is to attract distressed assets funds, to professionalize the management of such assets; however, this may be difficult given the hard discount these funds require and it may not be politically palatable.

Box 1.1   The Latvian Case: Proper Analysis Leads to Different Conclusions

Latvia's transition toward a market-based economy coupled with abundant liquidity, low interest rates—particularly on loans denominated in foreign currency—and the free flow of capital and labor following accession to the EU in 2004 led to a rapid expansion in largely foreign currency debt to individuals and corporates. The unwinding of this credit boom resulted in a deep recession, with GDP growth plummeting from double digits in 2007 to –18 percent in 2009 and nonperforming loans (NPLs) (those overdue by more than 90 days) exploding from 2 percent of loans at the start of the crisis to 19 percent by the end of 2010.

Ninety percent of individual loans and 70 percent of corporate loans were secured by real estate. Initial discussions about government intervention centered on a household mortgage debt restructuring scheme under which the government would guarantee repayments on a portion of a rescheduled mortgage for two years, in exchange for a partial debt write-off at the end if the loan was serviced on schedule. Opposed by banks as too costly and administratively burdensome, it also offered little relief to the poor, who typically did not have mortgages. Upon further review, the government recognized that direct government intervention in debt restructuring was not warranted. Deciding factors included the following:

- Household gross debt, although higher than in most other new EU members, was relatively low compared with that in countries in the euro area. The fact that mortgages were concentrated among higher-income households made it difficult to justify the use of public resources.
- There was little evidence of large-scale market failures that might hinder debt restructuring. The number of foreclosures had not resulted in a significant fall in real estate prices, as the participation in foreclosure auctions by the large banks' wholly owned asset management companies (AMCs) had established a floor on prices.
- The government's ability to intervene was severely limited by the available fiscal space and public debt sustainability concerns. Also, intervention might contravene EU rules limiting state aid to the private sector.
- The financial sector's problems were not systemic, and public funds were not at risk. The large Scandinavian banks accounted for 60 percent of the sector's assets and approximately 75 percent of mortgage lending. Their parents moved swiftly to provide an additional capital cushion to enable them to engage in the necessary restructurings or write-downs.
- The large banks also adopted a more socially responsible approach to resolving mortgage debt. Although speculative projects and second homes were subject to foreclosure, the banks attempted to work with households to maintain primary residences. Where foreclosure was the only option, banks generally entered into rental agreements in order to keep families in residences.

As a result, the authorities focused their efforts on facilitating a market-based restructuring process. Attention was paid to the need to facilitate voluntary out-of-court restructuring and refine insolvency legislation to support effective rehabilitation of viable firms. Specific reforms included the following:

- Amending tax legislation to strengthen the incentives for debt forgiveness
- Issuing guidelines for out-of-court corporate and consumer mortgage debt restructuring based on the London Approach and International Association of Restructuring, Insolvency, and Bankruptcy Professionals (INSOL)
- Expediting court approval of restructuring plans agreed to by the parties before the filing of a bankruptcy petition; lowering the threshold for initiating proceedings and the voting threshold for unsecured creditors to approve a rehabilitation plan; lengthening the rehabilitation period to a maximum of two years, to give financially distressed firms more time to restructure; and granting priority repayment status to creditors who provided new financing

These reforms were further complemented by strengthened regulation and supervision of the financial sector with (i) in-depth due diligence of all banks coupled with rigorous stress tests, followed by a bank-by-bank assessment of the appropriate measures to address potential capital shortfalls; (ii) new regulations on asset classification and provisioning, and implementation of the second pillar of Basel II; (iii) stronger liquidity and credit risk management regulations; and (iv) intensifying supervision, such as reporting on restructured loans. This case shows that a solid diagnostic is required to determine the most appropriate strategy and that a public AMC might not be the most suitable tool.

Source: M. Erbenova et al. (2011).

Overall, AMCs are most effective when part of multitrack restructuring solutions. There are certain assets that AMCs may not manage effectively, such as state-owned enterprises or strategic industries that may be politically sensitive. Small consumer loans are best managed by the originating financial institutions. Thus, AMCs work best when they are part of a multitrack approach to restructuring. Most of the AMCs studied were complemented by corporate restructuring frameworks and insolvency reforms (Korea, Indonesia, Malaysia, Turkey, and Ireland).

Commitment to Comprehensive Reforms

The political will to recognize the problem is the most critical precondition. Where credit losses have already occurred but are not recognized, it is usually very difficult for the government to face these losses, as it may entail fiscal costs to prevent banks from failing. However, in such a situation, time is of the essence: the longer it takes to recognize the problem, the larger the losses. The experience of Eastern Europe in the 1990s (in the Czech Republic and Slovakia) shows that it took a decade to design effective restructuring programs involving AMCs. The delays, however, opened room for substantial asset stripping, as evidenced by low recovery at auctions.

Political will should extend to a comprehensive package of reforms to address bank regulation and supervision, and resolution-impaired assets. Several successful AMCs were part of comprehensive solutions to restore financial stability (for example, Securum, Danaharta, and NAMA), which involved a strengthening of bank regulation and supervision, bank recapitalization programs, the creation of an AMC, and insolvency reforms, where warranted.

Systemic Crisis and Public Funds at Risk

A high level of NPLs is not a sufficient condition to establish a public AMC. Where banks are well capitalized but plagued with high NPLs, they should be able to withstand higher provisions, set up dedicated workout units, and draw on external expertise to solve their own problems. Regulation and supervision should be strengthened toward more conservative provisions and collateral valuation practices, and accelerated write-off standards. Likewise, if the problems are confined to one or more smaller banks, they should be addressed either by their shareholders or through the bank resolution process.

Weaknesses in the financial system should be systemic and put public funds at risk. Establishing an AMC is not warranted unless weaknesses in the financial system are systemic and threaten to put public funds at risk. The public AMC's role is to limit the ultimate cost to the public sector of resolving financial sector weaknesses, by recovering proceeds from assets that have lost value temporarily. Thus, the creation of a public AMC needs to be accompanied by a credible program to strengthen the banking sector through enhanced regulation and supervision as well as provisions to strengthen banks' capital positions where warranted.

In specific cases, purchases from "healthy institutions" may be warranted. Although participation in an AMC has generally been limited to insolvent banks or those recapitalized with public funds, the purchase of distressed assets from "healthy" banks (as in the case of Danaharta) or other financial institutions (as in the case of Korea's KAMCO) may be warranted to enhance confidence in the financial system, precluding the need for public funds in the future. It may also be needed to facilitate restructuring or disposition by consolidating multibank debt into one entity, or to create an efficient market for the sale of distressed assets.[1]

Solid Diagnostic and Critical Mass of Impaired Assets

A solid diagnostic of the banking system and impaired assets is a prerequisite to creating an AMC. Only such a diagnostic may assess the financial condition of the banks and whether an AMC may have a critical mass of homogenous assets to manage. This diagnostic is also necessary to determine the mandate of the AMC, either as a bank resolution entity if many institutions need to exit, or as an asset-purchasing entity in case most of them can continue operating. The diagnostic may reveal that the proportion of impaired assets is much higher than initially recognized by the banks (for instance, in Korea in March 1998, when the government applied internationally accepted standards to estimate the NPLs, the NPL ratio climbed from 5 to 18 percent).

The nonperforming assets should lend themselves to the recovery process. At a minimum, this means that the assets together with all rights and remedies are freely transferrable without the borrower's permission, and the underlying security is enforceable. The most attractive assets are loans secured by real estate or foreclosed real estate. Structured financial products such as collateralized debt obligations and other highly complex synthetic financial instruments do not lend themselves to more traditional recovery techniques and should not be transferred to an AMC. For instance in late 2009, a separate SPV was created to receive the toxic assets of the defunct German bank West LB, which included significant structured products.

To make a public AMC worthwhile, the nonperforming assets should have a critical mass. The workout process is costly and requires time and expertise. It is best implemented on large and complex loans. To expedite sales and attract professional buyers such as private equity funds, assets may have to be bundled according to common characteristics (hotels, commercial offices, and so forth). Thus, the ideal targets for AMCs are large and complex NPLs that can gain in value through the application of specialized expertise. For instance, Danaharta (Malaysia) removed about 70 percent of the banking sector's NPLs. The Sociedad de Gestión de Activos Procedentes de la Reestructuración Bancaria (SAREB; Spain) acquired about 40 percent in value of the real estate assets owned by banks.

Tradition of Institutional Independence and Public Accountability

To perform their duties, AMCs need institutional independence. An AMC is created within a local institutional framework and culture. As its business is prone to interference (it often must collect from politically connected parties), an AMC should enjoy strong protection from any third-party influence. One way to protect an AMC is to require transparency and accountability on its performance in its founding law. Countries that have a challenging governance environment and weak rule of law are not good candidates for a public AMC.

Robust Legal Framework for Bank Resolution, Debt Recovery, and Creditors' Rights

To protect the role of an AMC, the bank resolution framework should be clear about responsibilities and who bears the cost for bank resolution. An AMC is only a tool in the bank resolution framework and cannot replace the supervisory and resolution authorities (though in some cases, AMCs have played the role of resolution agency); nor should they absorb the permanent loss attributed to bank failure ("negative equity"). An AMC should be designed to absorb a temporary loss in the value of assets, which is expected to be offset within its lifetime by active asset management.

An AMC builds on a strong legal framework for creditors' rights. In many countries, AMCs were created because the legal framework for creditors' rights, asset securitization, and processes were deficient. As the necessary reforms could not be carried out in a timely manner, a public AMC was given special powers to deal with these constraints during its lifetime. These powers were also accompanied by reforms in insolvency and foreclosure laws so as to guarantee a level playing field for all financial institutions.

Efficient distressed-asset markets facilitate the role of an AMC. These include well-developed capital markets to securitize assets (as happened with KAMCO in Korea and the Resolution Trust Corporation (RTC) in the United States), deep real estate markets, and the existence of private AMCs. In some emerging markets (for instance, Korea and Turkey), foreign investors helped create distressed-asset markets. Turkey passed a law to enable private AMCs at the same time that the SDIF was retooled as a public AMC. Several local AMCs were established and partnered with firms with international experience (Deutsche Bank and Lehman, among others). These firms actively bid on and won the NPL portfolios sold by the SDIF. Private AMCs have played an important role in purchasing assets from public AMCs and then introducing proper workout practices into the local market.

Note

1. Public asset management companies (AMCs) are not appropriate in situations where the entire microfinance or financial cooperative sector is under stress, even though

many depositors may be at risk. This stems from the fact that AMCs need assets of a certain size and with certain characteristics in order to work them out cost-effectively; in the case of micro or small distressed loans, financial institutions would be best placed to restructure them, with the support of a dedicated workout unit or accelerated restructuring procedures. Consideration might also be given to global approaches featuring automatic rollover (maturity extensions) provisions, suitable grace periods, or payment moratoriums; or injection of liquidity into the sector for working capital.

CHAPTER 2

The Design: Legal and Institutional Framework

Mandate and Powers

What Should a Public AMC Do: Bank Resolution or Asset Management, or Both?

Public asset management companies (AMCs) have taken a variety of forms, with a focus on either bank resolution or asset management. Securum (Sweden), Danaharta (Malaysia), National Asset Management Agency (NAMA) (Ireland), and Sociedad de Gestión de Activos Procedentes de la Reestructuración Bancaria (SAREB) (Spain) are examples of AMCs with a narrow focus on asset management, restructuring, and disposition. They did not have responsibility for the resolution of failed banks: although Danaharta managed the assets of two failed banks for a fee, it was not involved in their closure or liquidation. Korea and Turkey chose to use existing entities for asset management. Turkey's Savings Deposit Insurance Fund (SDIF) and Indonesia's Indonesian Bank Restructuring Agency (IBRA) not only were responsible for the administration of blanket deposit guarantees, but also restructured and closed failed banks, and were responsible for recovering the losses caused by misuse of liquidity support by the former shareholders. Although the SDIF dealt only with the nonperforming loans (NPLs) of the institutions it managed, Indonesian private banks that were recapitalized jointly by the state and their shareholders were required to transfer their NPLs to IBRA. NAMA was allowed to purchase related-party performing loans so that they could control the restructuring of the entire relationship; unlike AMCON (the Asset Management Corporation of Nigeria), whose mandate was broadened to allow it to purchase performing loans deemed to be "systemically" important. Korea Asset Management Corporation (KAMCO) purchased NPLs from a variety of financial institutions, including merchant banks, insurance companies, and the like.

Successful AMCs had a narrow mandate with clearly defined goals. A focused mandate increases the chances of an AMC's success in meeting its objectives. Part of Securum's success was due to its narrow mandate of restructuring and selling the assets of two state-owned banks. It also benefited the coinciding strong economic recovery in the global markets as well as by introducing a more stable currency regime based on inflation targeting. The experience of SDIF and IBRA shows that their multiple mandates slowed the asset management function, as the entities spent their early years taking over and resolving failed banks.[1] Another challenge for these two entities was the confusion of roles with the bank supervisor which had to be clarified later. The Resolution Trust Corporation (RTC) was established as a bank resolution entity, but it benefited from deep and liquid capital markets to support asset sales. Unlike the RTC, IBRA and the SDIF had to place greater reliance on restructuring and to create a distressed-asset market through their sales. Thus, it is critical that the legal mandate of the AMC is specific and narrow, if possible, and that the AMC is allocated resources to fulfill its mandate.

Choices on mandate will depend on the diagnostic of the problem and the institutional structure for bank resolution. Asset management is a function that is needed when there is a large pool of similar assets whose value may be enhanced by effective management (for instance, a high level of real-estate-backed NPLs as for NAMA and SAREB, industrial assets as for Danaharta and Securum, or shareholders' loans for SDIF). By contrast, consider the portfolio of AMCON: 44 percent of which consisted of loans secured by shares and unsecured loans in 2014, which limits the need for active asset management as well as the recovery potential. An existing entity may implement asset management if it has the appropriate powers, as in the cases of the SDIF and KAMCO. In all cases, it is important to clarify up front the positioning of the AMC relative to the resolution and supervisory authorities. The AMC should not fill roles that are best played by other parties in the resolution process. This includes absorbing the permanent loss attributed to bank failure, which should be borne by the state. Absorbing such losses has made AMCON look financially unsustainable.[2]

How Should a Public AMC be Legally Established and Institutionalized?

AMCs can be established either as a statutory body under a specific law or as a limited liability company or corporation. The choice of legal entity depends on the country's legal tradition and system. In most common-law jurisdictions, a statutory body established under a law is preferred. This largely is due to the special powers given to the AMC; and may also be due to a need for the government to guarantee the bonds issued by the AMC to fund its NPL purchases, as in the case of Danaharta and AMCON. The special powers conferred also depend on what the legal system is for debt collection, insolvency, and creditors' rights, and especially asset management and securitization laws. A statutory body is also preferred in countries where the judicial system is stymied by delays and inefficiencies. However, a corporation may suffice when the legal system is efficient. Securum is an example of how a well-developed legal framework on foreclosure and insolvency allowed the AMC to be set up as an ordinary company under the finance company law.

AMCs need specific legislation to outline their mandate, powers, responsibilities, funding, and life span. The elaboration of the legislation also helps the authorities and the public form a consensus on the role of the entity. All newly established AMCs (except Securum) either had a dedicated law or had specific provisions included in the banking law. Even entities that were retooled to assume the function of asset management required specific legal provisions. Turkey's SDIF, a deposit insurance agency that existed before the crisis, was set up under the banking legislation, but amendments were required to enhance its special collection powers and autonomy. In Korea, KAMCO's broadened mandate on the acquisition and resolution of NPLs was granted by a dedicated law. The law should include at a minimum provisions on the mandate, the legal powers, the governance structure, the sunset clause, the funding, and the principles for determining the transfer price if the AMC is purchasing assets from financial institutions.

Specific legislation also protects AMCs against legal challenges. When an AMC acts as a resolution agency, its decisions should not be subject to being overturned by the court (the same as for the resolution authority). When an AMC purchases assets from open banks, it needs certainty about all possible legal actions outstanding against these assets. Buyers also request this certainty. Hence, the legislation should include provisions to terminate the ability of third parties to bring new legal actions with respect to pre-transfer activities after the transfer to the AMC. The legislation may incorporate a short period of time for borrowers to lodge such actions together with the AMC's ability to adjust the asset's purchase price after its evaluation of the merits of the claim. Also, any aggrieved party should be able to file a complaint with the court and obtain monetary damage. AMC legislation may also establish oversight committees to ensure the AMC does not abuse its special powers, as in the case of Danaharta in Malaysia.

Should an AMC be Publicly or Privately Owned?

The "public good" functions and public funding of AMCs call for establishing public institutions. As opposed to a bank-specific bad bank (for instance, RBS Capital Resolution in the United Kingdom or Grant Street Mellon in the United States), the public AMC carries a "public good" function for relieving the banking system of high nonperforming assets, and protecting depositors by preventing disorderly bank failure. Early AMCs reviewed here were fully owned by their government. Danaharta was a statutory corporation 100 percent owned by the Malaysian Ministry of Finance. Securum was a finance company fully owned by the Swedish government. More recently, AMCON is a public corporation fully owned by the Federal Government and Ministry of Finance of Nigeria.

In the European Union, there has recently been a drive to establish public-private AMCs. NAMA and SAREB were structured as majority privately owned AMCs, mostly to avoid consolidation into the national accounts which would put pressure on the public debt. For NAMA, this structure was implemented by setting up an SPV though which operations are conducted. SAREB is 55 percent

owned by the largest financial institutions in Spain (none of which has transferred assets to SAREB).

Private participation provides incentives for efficient management. Private
participation may reinforce the commercial focus of an AMC and facilitate its
work with the private sector. However, it is unlikely to be compatible with special
powers. The example of SAREB shows that an AMC may be set up as a private
company with a public mandate as long as it does not require special powers.

Regardless of public or private ownership, all AMCs should have a strong "commercial focus." They should be managed like commercial entities and strive to
obtain the best possible returns on the assets acquired while minimizing operating
costs so as to repay all their liabilities and pay back some, if not all, of their initial
equity (in face value).[3] On the basis of the experiences studied for this toolkit,
successful AMCs have repaid their bonds in full but not their initial capital.

Should AMCs have Special Powers?

Legislation is needed when an AMC is granted special powers. When the function of the AMC cannot be implemented within the existing legal framework,
specific legislation offers the advantage of recognizing that the AMC is an exceptional institution, established to resolve a specific problem (that is, a high level of
nonperforming assets), for which it may be granted special powers for a clearly
defined period of time.

Special powers override existing legislation. They include such provisions as the
ability to transfer loan assets into and out of the AMC without requiring the consent of the borrower; the power to transfer assets through statutory vesting; the
power of sale or sale by private treaty; the power to appoint a special administrator
to work out a settlement with secured creditors and facilitate the rehabilitation of
viable companies (as in the case of Danaharta in Malaysia, which was replicated
by AMCON in Nigeria); the power to obtain exemption from property tax and
stamp duties; and legal immunity for actions done in accordance with the law and
in good faith. By contrast, SAREB in Spain was established as a private company
and did not have special powers. However, a law was required to mobilize public
funding and to spell out the transparency requirements as well as a sunset clause.

Special powers should come with enhanced oversight. Because these powers
override existing legislation, they should be temporary and require higher levels of
governance and oversight to ensure that they are not abused. They may also lead to
market distortions that impede the ongoing resolution efforts of the banks. Examples
of special powers include such elements as the ability of the AMC, but not the
banks, to transfer assets without the borrower's consent; tax exemptions that lessen
the cost of buying an asset; and the ability of an AMC to attach unpledged assets
through an administrative rather than court procedure. In the case of the SDIF and
IBRA, many foreign banks refused to participate in the corporate restructuring
framework as they feared the AMC's special powers would place them at a disadvantage. Thus, it is critical that insolvency and foreclosure legislation is reformed at
the same time the AMC is established to ensure a level playing field with the banks.

What Should an AMC's General Powers Be?

An AMC should have the same creditors' rights as a selling bank. An AMC is expected to "step into the shoes" of the creditor, acquiring the same rights, including the set-off of claims and enforcement of collateral. Thus, the conditions of the loans or facilities should not change upon transfer to the AMC, such transfers may not give rise to any cause for action on the part of the borrower, and the borrower and guarantor remain fully responsible for meeting their obligations.

The general powers should be broad in relation to the assets. An AMC should have the capacity to restructure loans, including advancing fresh money (where warranted) to enable borrowers to restructure their businesses and ultimately repay their loans. It should be able to deal with recalcitrant borrowers and take any enforcement action permitted by the legal framework or participate in any secured creditors' workout. It should also be granted the ability to develop or enter into partnerships, joint ventures, and the like to develop partially completed real estate projects, if such development will enhance the recovery value. To ensure efficiency in dealing with assets and prevent undue borrower interference, the AMC's decisions with respect to its disposition activities should not be subject to unwinding by a court. Instead, if a court ultimately decides that the AMC did not have the right to sell the property, the borrower should be entitled to monetary damages rather than the return of the property.

Provision of equity capital is a debatable matter and it may be subject to misuse. Although entities, such as Securum, which engage in true corporate restructuring must gain ownership and control of companies to drive the restructuring process, for those AMCs engaged in financial restructuring and asset disposition, ownership of companies can prove problematic. Ownership positions may come about through debt-to-equity swaps or through entering into a commercial venture to develop unimproved property in the belief that it will provide a better return upon disposition. In these cases, extra care must be taken to ensure that the actions undertaken as owner do not unduly disadvantage other creditors. Managing equity positions requires a different skill set than managing NPLs and may require establishing a separate unit or fund staffed by investment professionals to oversee these investments. Finally, this power may be misused if an AMC is under pressure from authorities to maintain employment levels in distressed industries. An example is the AMCON legislation, which provides the power to invest in eligible equities (of any company), as defined by the central bank. This power led AMCON to acquire a discount house and equity in an airline and a car maker.

An AMC should have the ability to exercise its powers in conjunction with others. It may have to subcontract various asset management tasks such as loan collections and appoint receivers for its secured assets. It may also need to create subsidiaries or SPVs to ring-fence certain assets. KAMCO formed joint venture partnerships (typically with ownership split 50–50) with foreign investors to get their expertise in efficient management of NPLs and to prevent the intrusion of local domestic political pressure in the sale and purchase of NPLs. The RTC also made extensive use of joint venture partnerships to enable the sale of its less marketable property assets.

Scope

The issues of participation, eligible institutions, eligible assets, and transfer price are relevant only for AMCs that have purchased assets from open banks. They are not relevant for AMCs dealing only with the resolution of failed banks and their assets, such as the RTC and the SDIF. In such cases, the assets and sometimes the entire financial institutions were transferred to the AMC without the exchange of any consideration. Still, an AMC must establish its own valuation methodology to ensure that assets are carried on its books at their impaired value.[4] IBRA failed to do so with the result that early asset sales led to continuing losses, calling into question the AMC's efficiency. IBRA began to show recoveries only after assets were written down to their appropriate value.

Should Participation in an AMC Be Voluntary or Mandatory?

Experiences with voluntary private participation in AMCs are limited. The most successful example is provided by Danaharta; Bank Negara Malaysia issued a strong set of incentives to privately owned banks to sell assets to Danaharta (box 2.1). However, these incentives were highly focused on provisioning and may not be consistent with current International Financial Reporting Standards (IFRS).[5] The profit-sharing arrangements offer the benefit of aligning the incentives of the financial institutions with the AMC. However, they were not widely used in the case of Danaharta (under this scheme about 3 percent of all cash proceeds from purchased assets were redistributed to participating banks).

Box 2.1 Incentives from Bank Negara Malaysia for Danaharta

- All banks being recapitalized by Danamodel (the recapitalization agency) would have to sell their nonperforming loans (NPLs) to Danaharta.
- Banking institutions with a gross NPL ratio exceeding 10 percent were required to sell all their eligible NPLs to Danaharta; otherwise they would have to write down the value of these loans to 80 percent of the price offered by Danaharta. Danaharta made only one offer for each NPL.
- The Central Bank allowed banking institutions to amortize losses resulting from the sale to Danaharta for up to five years.
- Profit-sharing arrangements with selling institution were as follows: Danaharta shared any surplus recovery (after deducting recovery and holding costs) from the sale of the loans or assets, with the selling institutions receiving 80 percent of the surplus.
- Danaharta's bonds had a zero risk weight for capital adequacy purposes.

Source: Danaharta (2005).

Some AMCs had voluntary participation, but the uptake ended up coming solely from public banks. The genesis report of NAMA recommended a mandatory transfer from all banks. In the end, this was not required because all of the banks participating were either already nationalized or soon to be. Securum was open to all banks. The private banks, however, elected not to participate because the terms of public assistance were too onerous and the transfer price too low.

Mandatory participation schemes have relied on public support conditionality. Selling assets to the AMC was mandatory for all banks receiving public support in Malaysia, Indonesia, and Spain. This appears to be the most straightforward tool to drive private banks to sell assets to the AMC without infringing on property rights (by forcing banks to accept the transfer price of the AMC).

The banking supervisor has a role to play in devising incentives for participation in the AMC. The AMCON guidelines issued by the Central Bank of Nigeria mandated that three months from their entry into force, eligible financial institutions should not have more than 5 percent of their total loans classified as NPLs. This was very effective in ensuring the transfer of assets to AMCON. Such a decision, however, may preclude the AMC from effectively conducting its due diligence and will require provisions for a settlement period during which they can conduct their due diligence and adjust the pricing based on the results. Robust provisioning and accelerated write-offs standards are also an effective incentive and support financial stability:[6] if the bank has provisioned its loan to a value that is lower than the price offered by the AMC, it has an interest to sell to reverse the provision. The sale to the AMC also crystallizes the loss and removes the need for further write-downs and capital impairment; thus it is beneficial to both the shareholders and the supervisor.

Which Institutions Should be Eligible to Transfer Assets?

Because a public AMC may require the use of public funds to recapitalize one or more banks, the definition of eligible institutions should be carefully considered. The key criteria should be the systemic impact of eligible institutions; the total fiscal cost of the resolution (cost of capitalizing the AMC, guaranteeing bonds, and recapitalizing the eligible institutions following the transfer, if necessary); and the supervisory regime of eligible institutions. The supervision of eligible institutions, together with credit and risk management skills within the banks themselves, should be significantly strengthened after the transfer of assets to the AMC to prevent further origination of distressed assets.

Competition rules play a role in the eligibility of institutions. It may be difficult for a government to justify providing relief through the AMC to subsidiaries of perhaps well-capitalized foreign banks. At the same time, competition rules (such as EU competition law and the single market) may restrict the provision of state aid or may prohibit discriminatory treatment between domestic and foreign-owned institutions. The Irish authorities adopted a practical approach when NAMA was created: owing to the large indebtedness of the Irish government, they encouraged the subsidiaries of foreign banks to seek capital from their parent bank, and only come back to the government if they were not successful. In practice, none of the foreign subsidiaries solicited capital or participated in NAMA, although the act designates all credit institutions as eligible.

Eligible institutions should be solvent and viable after their asset transfer to the AMC. In the mandatory schemes, the asset transfer to the AMC was associated with recapitalization by the state. However, this principle is also relevant for entities that are not recapitalized with public funds. An AMC is an exceptional scheme to provide relief on the asset side by swapping non-earning assets for government-guaranteed securities. To prevent additional fiscal cost, the financial supervisor should ensure that eligible institutions have adequately provisioned for all their assets and have capital buffers. In practice, the recapitalization of institutions by public or private funds due to the reevaluation of assets should happen at the same time as the transfer (in the case of SAREB in Spain) or before.

Nonbank financial institutions have rarely participated in AMCs. The RTC was established to address multiple failings of savings and loans associations but these were quasi banks. KAMCO is the exception: it was allowed to acquire NPLs from all types of financial institutions (banks, trust investment companies, insurance companies, merchant banks, and securities companies). This was because Korea had a more diversified financial system than other Asian countries, and because of the severity of the crisis in the corporate sector, which was exposed to a variety of financial institutions. To determine whether nonbanks should participate, the fiscal cost implications, the systemic feature of the institutions, and the composition of assets should be examined.

Which Assets Should be Eligible to be Transferred to an AMC?

An AMC should purchase assets for which it has a clear comparative advantage. Purchases should be restricted to large, complex assets in need of financial and operational restructuring for which banks do not have capacity. The purchase of retail NPLs should be avoided because of the high cost of collecting these low-value loans. The number of assets purchased increases the operating cost. NAMA and Danaharta ended up with about 3,000 assets versus 12,000 for SAREB. Restricting the number of assets purchased in both number and value[7] requires a good inventory and detailed analysis of the distressed assets prior to the establishment of the AMC. The AMC should have the right to put back or adjust the price of assets if the security has not been correctly perfected.

Certain complex assets such as state-owned enterprises or strategic industries should not be handled by an AMC. These assets may expose an AMC to political interference and prevent it from fulfilling its mandate on other assets. Instead, for such assets, other restructuring tracks should be implemented. These entities may be restructured by a separate agency such as a state holding company or privatization agency. Or the AMC may establish a separate sub-sidiary and outsource the restructuring of state-owned enterprises to a private professional partner (as in the case of the Czech Republic in the late 1990s; box 2.3).

The purchase of performing assets should have a clear rationale. Twenty per-cent of the loans purchased by NAMA were performing, because it acquired all the connected loans from one single borrower. In the early years, these loans provided much-needed cash before the receipt of recoveries. In addition, they have facilitated the resolution of loans as the borrower has had to deal with only one entity. This is in contrast to SAREB, which did not choose to consolidate a borrower's entire relationship and has experienced difficulties in dealing with multiple lenders. The concept was applied differently by AMCON, which pur-chased large performing loans from banks on the grounds that they were sys-temically important. This was interpreted by some as a political gesture. Overall, it makes sense to purchase performing loans if they are linked to the NPLs so as to deal with all the facilities of a particular borrower, but an AMC should not purchase unconnected performing loans. Performing borrowers need a banking relationship, and their business may be irreparably harmed by their transfer to an AMC.[8]

How Should the Price of the Assets Purchased be Determined?

A thorough process of asset valuation before the transfer of assets is a key success factor. The lower the purchase price, the easier for an AMC to recover the pur-chase price, together with all expenses, and show financial success but the higher the capital deficiency of the selling institution. These two competing elements must be carefully balanced by a thorough asset valuation process. The valuation can take many forms: it may result from the due diligence of the AMC (Danaharta, NAMA), or from a generalized diagnostic on the banking sector (called an asset quality review, or AQR, at SAREB). When an AMC is being considered, there may not be time for real estate appraisals and on-site inspec-tion of the collateral. The appraisal standards may not be strong enough to pro-vide confidence in the values. However, failure to conduct a thorough, indepen-dent valuation exercise may result in an AMC overpaying for assets and not being able to show recoveries. As valuation is an art and not an exact science, a mechanism for posttransfer price adjustments, such as hybrid bonds, should be included in the design of the AMC. However, these features need to be designed carefully to ensure that they meet the criteria for a "true sale" and the regulator is likely to require that they be fully written off due to their contingent nature.[9] An AMC should also have the right to return a loan to a financial institution within a certain period of time, should it not meet the eligibility criteria. Owing to time constraints, SAREB purchased assets at an average discount; however, it had to implement in-depth due diligence afterwards to value individual assets and ensure appropriate valuation and provisions. All AMCs should periodically review and reevaluate their assets.

Public Asset Management Companies • http://dx.doi.org/10.1596/978-1-4648-0874-6

The value of the assets should be established through a transparent, market-based, due diligence process conducted by an independent third party experienced in valuation. This is regardless of whether the AMC or the supervisor is in charge of determining the transfer price, as neither entity may have the skills to conduct asset valuations. The independent valuation also provides a level of protection for the institution, as well as assurances to the public that the valuation process was fair and unbiased. In Ireland, NAMA led the valuation process and performed legal reviews and property valuations using a model developed by external financial advisers. Then an external firm, acting as audit coordinator, reviewed all loan valuations and certified the consistency of the process (box 2.2). In Spain, the Bank of Spain (BoS) determined the transfer price on the basis of an independent asset valuation of the banking system, according to criteria set out in the royal decree establishing SAREB.[10] The process followed by AMCON was less robust: it purchased assets backed by real estate at the average of the open-market valuation and the forced-sale valuation provided by the eligible institution, and that price was subject to reevaluation within 12 months by a reputable appraiser jointly appointed by AMCON and the financial institution. The valuation process was not transparent, as the transfer price was not disclosed and no comprehensive independent review was carried out to ensure that appraisals were consistent.[11]

Box 2.2 NAMA Valuation Process

- Participating banks identified the eligible assets and provided National Asset Management Agency (NAMA) with information about the loans and borrowers using standard templates provided by NAMA.
- The information included legal due diligence reports, current market valuations of properties pledged as collateral for loans, and information about security, other than real estate, pledged as collateral by borrowers.
- The valuation date specified by the NAMA Board was November 30, 2009.
- NAMA validated the information through legal reviews, property valuation reviews, and valuation of financial derivative contracts.
- Loan valuers, using a model developed by financial advisors, calculated a long-term value for each loan, taking into account the value of the loan collateral (after uplift for long-term economic value) and the current market value of non–real estate collateral. Adjustments were made to take account of due diligence and enforcement costs likely to be incurred by NAMA.
- A firm acting as audit coordinator reviewed all loan valuations and certified whether they had been accurately calculated in accordance with the valuation model and whether the valuations of real estate collateral had been determined on a consistent basis in accordance with criteria determined by NAMA.

Source: NAMA Comptroller and Auditor General (2010).

If a generalized diagnostic of a banking system's assets (an AQR) is used to determine the transfer price, various design elements should be in place. Usually the AQR is used for supervisory purposes, to assess the adequacy of capital and provisions. If it is also used to determine the transfer price, the methodology should have the following features: it should be transparent and disseminated by the supervisory authority, to facilitate the acceptability of the transfer price; it should include sample checks on the quality of the collateral values (with physical appraisals), and perfection of security, as well as enforcement rights; the AMC should have the right to adjust the price based on market conditions, holding costs and perfection of security interests; and the price should be valid only for a limited time.

In all cases, the transfer price should reflect the market value of the assets. The concept of long-term economic value applied in Spain and Ireland is unlikely to be appropriate for most emerging markets. This concept means that in the absence of current market values for pricing assets, such assets could be valued at their "real economic value," based on observable market inputs and realistic and prudent assumptions about future cash flows.[12] The concept implies that market conditions have temporarily disappeared for some categories of assets. In practice, NAMA and SAREB applied an uplift factor to the transfer price assessed through new collateral valuation (NAMA) or an AQR (SAREB). For NAMA, the uplift was 8.3 percent on average and assumed that real estate markets would recover over time. Use of this technique requires a well-established property market with demonstrated long-term historical average prices. It is not appropriate when property markets are underdeveloped and historical average prices are not clearly documented. It should never be used to avoid proper loss recognition. Even in cases where the information is available, use of this technique may lead to overpaying for the assets: NAMA considers that it overpaid for its assets by some €5.6 billion. In addition, it absorbed another €4.5 billion loss in value due to a 25–30 percent decline in the property market after the property collateral valuation date. In total, NAMA estimates that it overpaid the banks on the transaction date by about €10 billion.

How Should Assets be Effectively Purchased?

Using a vesting order as a legal instrument to transfer assets to an AMC is effective and fast. Use of a vesting order automatically places an AMC in the shoes of the original lender. All rights and liabilities of the lender are automatically assumed by the AMC, eliminating the necessity for individual transfer of titles, charges, and securities. In addition, a vesting order provides that the AMC takes title to the assets free and clear of all encumbrances and claims and in a manner that is approved by the law. Thus, the AMC can be assured that no creditor will "lie in the weeds" or subsequently lay claim to the assets or any part thereof. A vesting order also provides certainty in that it makes it very difficult to challenge the transfer once the order is made in accordance with the law. It is also often the only means available to transfer the assets of an unwilling or insolvent party. All transfers of assets to and from Danaharta were done through vesting orders.

Governance and Funding

Why is Good Governance Important and How to Promote it?

Distressed-asset management is a business highly prone to corruption. In many countries, markets for distressed assets are not readily available to facilitate price disclosure. The uncertainty in the value of assets may give rise to non-transparent practices. As an AMC effectively establishes a market for distressed assets, it benefits from a robust governance, ethics, and transparency framework that protects the public purse. It is also critical to protect an AMC in its dealings with high-profile borrowers. As a result of its size, an AMC can play a leading role in changing certain business practices (as in the case of NAMA, which professionalized the real estate market in Ireland). Good governance and independence protects an AMC and allows it to carry out its mandate effectively.

Governance provisions in an AMC's law are necessary, but practices matter more. Legal provisions on the composition, term, appointment, and removal of the board and key management staff should be clearly spelled out in the founding act. Fit and proper criteria, relevant experience, and declarations of interest should be required of board members and key management. Board members should be required to disclose all possible conflicts of interest and to recuse and absent themselves from all discussions regarding these subjects. The founding law should also spell out the responsibilities of the board as well as the establishment of key committees such as the audit committee. The IBRA case shows the difficulty of enforcing good governance when the law is silent. However, the law may have sound provisions but poor implementation, as in the case of the Czech Revitalization Agency (box 2.3). In reality, an AMC is set up within a specific

---

Box 2.3 Czech Revitalization Agency: Good Design Overwhelmed by Poor Implementation

In the fall of 1997, the Czech Republic experienced a full-scale banking crisis. In June 1998, the new government quickly agreed that privatization was the most cost-effective means of dealing with the ailing sector. Serious disagreements arose with respect to revitalizing the distressed industrial conglomerates, with two versions of a plan called "Revitalization of Czech Enterprises" being proposed. The first, promoted by the minister of industry and trade, involved massive subsidies, soft loans, tax breaks, and credit guarantees to prop up large, debt-ridden industrial corporations. It would effectively have recapitalized one of the largest banks by recapitalizing some of its largest debtors. It was strongly opposed by the deputy prime minister for economic policy and the minister of finance, on the grounds of the staggering financial cost, obvious moral hazard, and rent-seeking behavior by bank creditors and corporate shareholders.

box continues next page

Box 2.3   Czech Revitalization Agency: Good Design Overwhelmed by Poor Implementation *(continued)*

In April 1999, a compromise revitalization program was adopted that aimed to recapitalize a few significant companies through the use of strategic investors. The Revitalization Agency was established as a wholly owned subsidiary of the Czech Consolidation Bank (KOB), a financial institution owned by the Ministry of Finance, established for the purpose of managing state assets. The agency had a mandate to select potentially viable, large, distressed companies for its portfolio, purchasing their debt or equity at fair market value, managing and restructuring these assets to minimize fiscal costs, and maximizing revenues from asset sales through competitive tenders. In an attempt to protect the agency from political interference as well as increase its efficiency, key design features included the following:

- *Outsourced management*: A reputable international investment firm was chosen through a transparent, open bidding process to manage the entity and oversee the restructuring. Its remuneration was based on a combination of an annual retainer and fees related to restructuring work on the portfolio companies following the adoption of restructuring plans. The company-specific fees were based on a mixture of monthly advisory fees and success fees for completed restructuring transactions. To ensure the manager was motivated by successful outcomes, monthly fees were credited against success fees.
- *Executive Board*: Consisting of five members, three appointed by the manager and two by KOB, this board had decision-making authority. Prior approval by a supermajority of the Investment Committee was required for restructuring plans and amendments, as well as transactions exceeding CZK 50 million.
- *Independent Investment Committee*: Charged with the approval of the restructuring proposals submitted by the manager, the committee consisted of nine members, including the Executive Board members and four outsiders recruited from the ranks of independent workout or financial specialists. Effectively, the committee was designed to prevent and resolve conflicts between the parties, especially KOB and the manager, while providing an objective, independent assessment of the restructuring plans, including the remuneration of the manager in the context of individual restructuring plans.
- *Supervisory Board*: Consisting of nine government appointees, this board was responsible for monitoring the agency's activities but could not change or amend restructuring plans or transactions.
- *Eligibility criteria*: To ensure a manageable number of viable companies, participants had to meet minimum levels of employment, volume of goods and services bought from domestic suppliers, and loans outstanding, and to have been earnings before interest, taxes, depreciation, and amortization (EBITDA) positive in the preceding accounting period. They also had to agree to participate and accept the prospect of a substantial dilution of their equity position.

box continues next page

Box 2.3 Czech Revitalization Agency: Good Design Overwhelmed by Poor Implementation *(continued)*

Before the agency could purchase assets, the government recapitalized the state-owned banks by transferring large volumes of nonperforming loans (NPLs) to KOB at inflated prices. As the agency could acquire NPLs only at fair market value, which would have required KOB to recognize an immediate loss—a political impossibility for the government—the agency could not gain effective control of the companies and was relegated to an advisory role. A political feud ensued between the proponents of the plan, which led to the dissolution of the agency.

Lessons learned: A key objective of the agency's design was to shield its operations from political interference and pressures from special interest groups through good governance, transparency, and professional management. These elements, well regarded by international financial and development institutions, proved insufficient in the face of a lack of consensus and political will as reflected in the unwillingness to recognize the full extent of the losses in the banks and to adequately fund the agency.

Source: M. Sanders (2006).

---

country's legal, institutional, and cultural framework, and extra care must be taken to ensure that it does not fall prey to the same weak practices that produced the need for an AMC.

Some practices have been developed to strengthen good governance. The case studies show that the best-performing AMCs have been the ones with the strongest governance practices.

These have included the appointment of international experts on the board (as was done for Danaharta, NAMA, and IBRA, or as advisers to the board; the adoption and publication of key performance indicators (KPIs) to measure the success of the AMC (Danaharta); internal staff rules requiring that all communications that attempt to influence staff be reported to the board (SAREB). AMCs may also benefit from periodic progress evaluations conducted by outside parties.

Robust transparency requirements and external controls strengthen governance. They help cast public scrutiny on an AMC to ensure it meets its mandate and targets. The AMC law should include requirements for the publication of annual audited accounts, audit by an independent third party or public body if relevant (national audit office), publication of quarterly and other medium-term reports on the AMC's performance, and regular hearings by the legislature. All these reports should be readily available on an AMC's website, and management should communicate publicly on the AMC's performance.

An AMC should follow internationally accepted accounting standards ("IAS"). If an AMC is created as a statutory body, it may have to follow public accounting rules. However, these rules may fall short of guidance and transparency about the valuation of distressed assets once transferred. Another option is to follow the same rules in force by the financial institutions from which the AMC purchases the assets. NAMA follows IFRS, but SAREB's accounting rules are determined by the BoS, its supervisor, and also the rule-making body for the implementation of IFRS for banks and financial entities in Spain.

How Much Money Does an AMC Need?

The funding structure differs depending on whether an AMC is tasked with purchasing assets from open banks or resolving failed banks. An asset-purchasing AMC will need an initial capitalization for working capital and the absorption of future losses on the assets. It may issue government-guaranteed securities to purchase the distressed assets and would have to pay the interest on the bonds from the collection proceeds. A resolution AMC will use working capital to manage and sell the assets, and may also be tasked with absorbing the losses when the transfer of deposits to acquirers is not matched by sufficient good assets (as with the RTC and the SDIF). If an AMC is acting as a receiver once deposits have been transferred, the working capital should be paid out of the assets of the bank in receivership (as in the case of Danaharta for the managed assets).

The initial capital should be tailored to the cash needs and timing of expected collections. The cash needs of an AMC follow a descending curve (figure 2.1). At the beginning of its life, an AMC will require cash to pay for the interest on its bonds (for a purchasing AMC) and the management of the assets. Significant cash collections should begin no later than year three, and the AMC should then be able to generate sufficient funds to meet its working capital needs. The bonds

Figure 2.1 Typical Cash Used over AMC Lifetime (Asset-Purchasing)

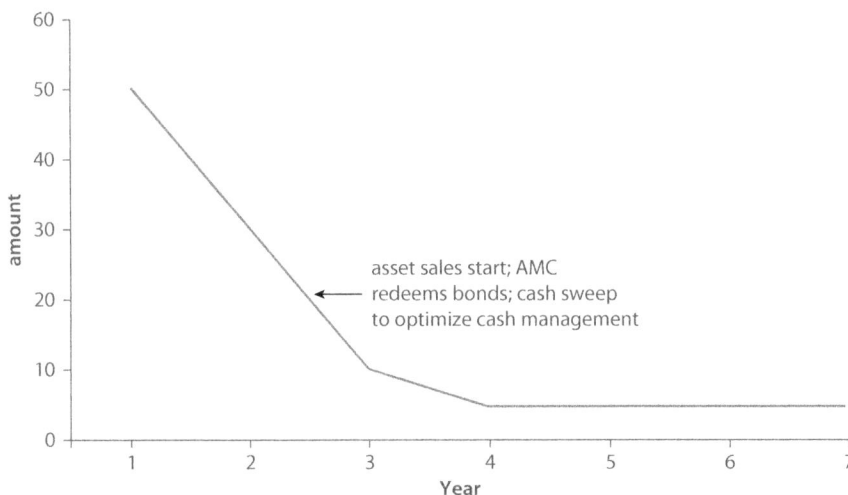

Source: World Bank.
Note: AMC = asset management company.

issued by an AMC should have prepayment features, or cash sweep/sinking funds to avoid the build-up of excess cash, which may lead the AMC to make imprudent investments.

Predictability in the funding process is a key success factor. The RTC's periodic lack of funding severely hampered its resolution efforts, forcing it to place banks in conservatorship for extended periods of time and to place greater emphasis on selling assets rather than institutions. The SDIF also experienced undue delays in funding, which resulted in increased losses as illiquid and insolvent banks were kept open and proved vulnerable to interest rate shocks. To ensure smooth operations, the law should include provisions and all necessary appropriations for not only the initial capital but also the working capital, to ensure that the AMC has sufficient resources to support its operations until internal cash flow turns positive.

How Should an AMC Pay for the Assets Purchased?

Asset-purchasing AMCs have issued a variety of government-guaranteed bonds in exchange for the assets. The two main options have been zero coupon bonds (where the bond is issued at a discount and redeemed at par, including the accrued coupon) and regular coupon bonds. The zero coupon bond limits the pressure on an AMC's cash in early years. However, the eligible institutions must be strong enough to forgo a regular income stream while the bond is outstanding. Most securities issued have been bullet bonds, with prepayment clauses. The maturity of the bonds was generally matched with the AMC's life span, and the interest rate was determined on the basis of the government yield curve.

The bonds should be discountable at the central bank to obtain liquidity assistance. The purpose of an AMC is not only to enhance the asset quality of eligible institutions but also to provide liquidity to restart credit intermediation. Zero coupon bonds, however, do not provide a regular cash (liquid) stream for the eligible institutions. The banks may be experiencing credit needs in excess of that provided by the income stream from the bonds. In these cases, banks should be able to discount the bonds at the central bank to obtain the required liquidity. NAMA and SAREB's bonds are eligible collateral at the European Central Bank. AMCON's bonds are discountable at the Central Bank of Nigeria. In some countries, however, the central bank may not be able to accept collateral issued by (majority) privately owned entities, so such limitation should be taken into account when designing the AMC.

Safeguards Mechanisms and Supervision

Safeguards mechanisms apply to all types of AMCs. They aim to protect the taxpayers against future liabilities created by an AMC if it does not perform financially or strays from its mandate. There are two types of safeguards: time-limit safeguards to ensure an AMC acts expeditiously and financial safeguards to avoid it becoming a fiscal burden. Financial transparency already plays the role of safeguard when there is a free press and a financial community that can assess the performance of an AMC. Hence it is desirable to add safeguards to AMCs in countries that have weak legal and institutional environments. However, safeguards should be tailored so as not to unduly limit the effectiveness of an AMC. In environments of weak governance and rule of law, the preconditions for an AMC should be assessed thoroughly, as safeguards may improve practices but not counter fundamental trends.

Is a Sunset Clause Needed? And a Time Limit on the Purchase of Assets?

A sunset clause is critical to focus the mandate of an AMC and to protect the public purse. Most of the AMCs reviewed had a sunset clause whether they purchased assets or acted as resolution entities. The sunset period varied in length from 5 to 15 years, depending on the type of assets purchased, and some AMCs had their mandate cut short from what was initially envisaged.[13] The lack of a sunset clause increases the risk of mission creep, whereby an AMC may be called on to resolve any financial or commercial entity, or the entity may morph into a development entity, thereby increasing the cost for the taxpayers. Consistent with the sunset clause, the time to purchase assets should also be limited: the sooner an AMC gets the assets on its books, the sooner it can work them out and collect. This reinforces the exceptional feature of an AMC and gives a strong signal to financial institutions to recognize losses.

There are exceptions for entities that are retooled to perform the function of asset management. The SDIF and KAMCO were pre-existing entities that were given the function of asset management during banking crises. They did not have sunset clauses. However, they were under intense public scrutiny to perform their mandate and sold most of their assets within six years. Some provisions also required them to act expeditiously: for instance, the reform of the SDIF legislation required it to resolve a bank within a maximum of 12 months. And KAMCO's ability to purchase assets and issue bonds was limited to five years.

Which Financial Safeguards?

Financial safeguards may not be necessary if the role of an AMC can be appropriately assessed by the local financial community and external controllers. Such safeguards could take the following features: an overall limit on the total debt issued by the AMC (SAREB) or total borrowing; a requirement that the AMC remain solvent; an equity-to-asset ratio. The limit on total debt is a good incentive to cap the size of the AMC at inception and prevent mission creep. The leverage and equity ratios are a double-edge sword. They may promote sound financial management of the AMC; however, if they cannot be met, the AMC may lose credibility.[14] Financial safeguards may be counterproductive and best replaced by restrictions on the use of the cash (sinking funds for the bonds, repayment clauses) and financial transparency.

Should an AMC be Supervised by a Financial Supervisor?

Supervision by a financial supervisor is a debatable issue. Where financial institutions are exposed to AMC bonds that are not guaranteed by the government, the financial supervisor must ensure that the AMC remains financially sound and does not pose a risk for the financial system. However, the financial supervisor may not be equipped to understand and supervise an AMC. Bringing an AMC under financial supervision may send a message that it is a permanent part of the financial landscape whereas it is designed to be an exceptional tool. Of the AMCs reviewed, only SAREB and AMCON are supervised by the central bank. The SDIF was initially under the authority of the banking supervisor, then provided with formal independence together with stronger governance.

Notes

1. The Savings Deposit Insurance Fund's (SDIF, Turkey) success in loan collections was primarily due to the shareholders' loans (91 percent of all nonperforming loan (NPL) recoveries), for which it had special collection powers. By contrast, 87 percent of Indonesian Bank Restructuring Agency (IBRA's) NPL sales occurred in the last two years of its existence (2002–4).

2. In Turkey, the SDIF was initially tasked with absorbing the negative equity and recapitalizing the banks before selling them; however, in 2008, the Treasury cancelled the SDIF's debt in recognition of the fact that these costs are more properly a burden of the state.

3. Recent asset management companies (AMCs) have been highly leveraged to provide the returns that investors require. For instance, Sociedad de Gestión de Activos Procedentes de la Reestructuración Bancaria (SAREB's) senior debt at inception was 42 times the equity, or 11 times the equity and subordinated notes.

4. All AMCs should keep two sets of records. One records the legal obligation of the borrower, while the second records the impaired or book value of the asset.

5. Under IAS 39, the amount of loss (and thus provision) is measured as the difference between the asset's carrying amount and the present value of estimated future cash flows (excluding future losses not incurred), discounted at the original interest rate. A requirement to value the asset at 80 percent of the price offered by the AMC would be unlikely to be compatible with such a valuation method.

6. For instance, a prudential requirement that after a certain time past due the loan be written off or that risk weights be raised on impaired assets beyond a certain vintage.

7. As shown in the attached case studies, approximately 80 percent of the AMCs values were centered on 20 percent of their assets by number. Those AMCs that restricted their purchases to these larger assets were more successful.

8. In the case of an AMC that is tasked with resolving failed banks, every attempt should be made to transfer performing loans to another bank as quickly as possible. Where this is not possible, consideration may be given to allowing one bank to remain open to provide essential banking functions for these borrowers until they can establish a new banking relationship.

9. National Asset Management Agency (NAMA) issued 5 percent of the purchase price of its assets in the form of subordinated debt payable only if certain performance targets are met. The banks were required by the supervisor to write this debt off.

10. Royal Decree 1559/2012 (chapter 3), of November 15, 2012, established the framework for AMCs. The independent valuation carried out by Oliver Wyman focused on 14 banking groups, accounting for 90 percent of all domestic credit in the financial system.

11. Asset Management Corporation of Nigeria (AMCON) Guidelines, Schedule 1.

12. European Commission, Communication from the European Commission on the Treatment of Impaired Assets in the Community Banking Sector, 2009/C 72/01.

13. Securum's life span was cut from 15 to 6 years and the Resolution Trust Corporations (RTC's) from 7 to 6 years.

14. For instance, SAREB had negative equity as of end 2014, which was due to the valuation of the interest rate swaps and impairment provisions. SAREB has been working with the BoS on a new accounting standard that would allow the AMC to register only net losses (set off incurred gains and incurred losses—information as of August 2015).

CHAPTER 3

Building Effective Operations in an AMC

With the passage of the enabling legislation, control of an asset management company (AMC) passes from policy makers to its directors and key officers. Although an AMC may have been shaped by the policy decisions embedded in the legislation, much work lies ahead to ensure that it operates efficiently and effectively. Though policy makers should not participate in operations, they need to have a general idea of key operational issues so that they can more effectively design and then judge an AMC's performance and provide support where warranted.

Three areas are of key importance to ensuring the effective and efficient operation of an AMC. These are organization and staffing; asset management, including strategic planning; and internal controls and transparency. In addition, as AMCs are temporary, self-liquidating entities, their closure should be adequately planned in advance.

Organization and Staffing

When Should the Planning Process begin and Who Should be Responsible?

Planning should begin as soon as the decision to establish an AMC has been made. Responsibility for this work may be assigned to an interagency task force (NAMA, RTC), the Ministry sponsoring the AMC [the Ministry of Finance (MOF) in the case of IBRA] or by the existing entity which will assume the duties of the AMC (KAMCO). Personnel should be assigned to the project on a full-time basis, and the team should have direct access to high-level decision makers to resolve interagency issues, should they arise, and to make key decisions, particularly with respect to recovery strategies.

The length of the planning process has varied greatly depending on both the strength of consensus among the authorities and the mandate. In the case of

KAMCO, which benefited from a strong consensus and narrow mandate, eight months elapsed from the time that the AMC concept was raised until it purchased its first assets. In Indonesia, which lacked these two critical elements, it took over a year.

What is the Role of the Board of Directors?

The AMC is overseen and governed by its board of directors. The board should not be involved in the day-to-day running of the organization. Rather, its principal responsibility is to provide the necessary leadership to ensure that the AMC fulfills its mandate in an efficient and effective manner. Its principal role is to set the strategic objectives and targets for the organization and ensure that appropriate systems, procedures, and resources are in place to achieve the objectives.

How Big Should the Board be and Who Should Sit on it?

AMC boards have generally consisted of between 7 and 11 members, the majority of whom have come from the public sector. Exceptions include Securum and NAMA, whose boards are primarily composed of individuals from the private sector. The chief executive officer (CEO) of the AMC is generally an ex officio member of the board. Both Danaharta and NAMA also included one board member with international experience in asset management.

The Ministry of Finance or Treasury is most commonly represented on the board. Other common appointments have included representatives of the central bank, the financial sector regulator, and the deposit insurer. IBRA chose to include the secretary of the Financial Sector Policy Committee in place of either the central bank or regulator. The secretary of housing and urban development was included on the RTC oversight board, in line with its social mandate to provide affordable housing.

Private sector board members have been chosen by a variety of methods. In the case of both IBRA and the RTC, the private sector members were appointed by the president, although RTC appointees were also subject to the advice and consent of the Senate. The chairman of the Korean Federation of Banks appointed two bankers to KAMCO's board, and KAMCO's CEO chose three additional members from the private sector, including an attorney-at-law, a certified public accountant (CPA) or a certified tax accountant, and a university professor or research professional. NAMA used a more innovative approach to board selection, holding an open competition in which any experienced individual with no ties to the financial crisis was eligible to apply. The minister of finance, however, did have the flexibility to choose someone who had not applied.

What is the Role of Board Committees?

The board is generally assisted in its work by one or more committees, the most important of which is the Audit Committee. Although the exact names, functions, and number of committees will vary with the AMC's mandate, the committees commonly include the following:

- *Audit Committee*: assists in the oversight of financial reporting as well as the independence and integrity of the internal and external control processes. The internal audit function reports directly to the Audit Committee, to ensure its independence. NAMA's Audit Committee is also responsible for monitoring the compliance of the banks with the terms of their loan servicing contracts.
- *Credit Committee*: operates under delegated authority from the board, which has ultimate responsibility for the credit risk of the AMC's portfolio. The Credit Committee is responsible for approving or rejecting those transactions (loan restructuring terms, asset sales, loaning additional amounts, and the like), which fall below the level required for board approval but exceed the credit approval authority delegated to the management by the board.
- *Finance and Operating Committee*: monitors the financial and operational management of the AMC, including its performance against budgetary indicators and KPIs. It may exercise oversight of the procurement process and of certain key service providers such as appraisers, legal services, and so on.
- *Risk Management Committee*: oversees the implementation of board-approved risk management policies as well as the ongoing review and oversight of the risk profile of the AMC within the context of approved risk policy.
- *Personnel Committee*: assists the board in establishing personnel, compensation, and benefit policies and practices; in employee relations; as well as in staffing levels and organizational structure.

The board may also wish to establish one or more advisory or technical committees. These committees, composed of directors and external experts, are designed to keep the board abreast of more technical issues (such as valuation methodologies and market conditions) that may affect the AMC's ability to accomplish its goals. The RTC was mandated by law to establish 12 regional advisory boards, to ensure greater private sector input, particularly with respect to conditions in the real estate sector. NAMA established two such committees: a planning advisory committee to provide input on planning, land, and related matters that may affect the value and disposition of NAMA's assets and a committee to advise on matters with respect to the agency's portfolio in Northern Ireland.[1]

Where Should the AMC be Located?

AMCs are traditionally located in a country's capital city. The only exception to this has been the Savings Deposit Insurance Fund (SDIF, Turkey), which is headquartered in Istanbul, the Turkish financial center. Depending on the size of the country and the geographic distribution of assets, AMCs have established one or more regional offices. The RTC had the most extensive branch network, with 4 regional offices, 14 consolidated offices, and 14 sales centers.

Public Asset Management Companies • http://dx.doi.org/10.1596/978-1-4648-0874-6

How are AMCs Organized?

Most AMCs have been organized along functional lines, as dictated by their mandate. AMCs with broad mandates have tended to be organized in units that focus on bank restructuring, asset management or servicing, and, in the case of both IBRA and the SDIF, shareholder recoveries. NAMA is organized in five main units: finance, including support operations; property development; strategy and communications; legal; and asset recovery and traditional workout activities. Securum chose to organize functionally, reflecting the nature of the underlying assets, with units responsible for the management and disposal of loans, real estate assets, equity positions, industrial assets, and international assets. The RTC, which relied heavily on outsourcing the servicing of its loan portfolio, focused its organizational structure on its sales efforts and management of the servicing agents.

How are AMCs Staffed?

AMCs require staff with a wide variety of skills. Many AMCs established during a systemic banking crisis have relied heavily on employing staff from the closed or restructured banks (IBRA, the SDIF). Although bankers can be used to service the nonperforming loan (NPL) portfolio, a successful AMC requires staff with a wider variety of skill sets. These include marketing; in-depth industry experience, including turnaround skills, if engaged in corporate restructuring; investment banking; construction management; portfolio valuation (including appraisers); and legal expertise.

All AMCs grapple with staff remuneration and retention issues. As the AMC staff is essentially working itself out of a job, their compensation should reflect this lack of job security. For many countries this has proved to be problematic. Given the public nature of the AMC, it is difficult to justify wages that are higher than those of civil servants, particularly if the government has been forced to reduce the pay of civil servants to meet fiscal constraints. And as the economy improves, the most qualified staff members will seek more permanent positions. Retention bonuses have proven helpful in such situations, as have bonuses linked to the attainment of KPIs (Danaharta). NAMA introduced a voluntary redundancy scheme for nonessential staff to provide for a more orderly downsizing of its staff.

Outsourcing may prove to be a partial solution to staffing issues. As temporary entities, AMCs should strive for lean organizational structures and aim to outsource as many functions as possible. Payroll and IT functions such as data processing and archives are just a few of the activities which can be outsourced. Outsourcing the servicing of NPL portfolios, particularly consumer loan portfolios, should be considered. In those markets where these services are not readily available from domestic companies, external (or foreign) servicing options should be explored. In the case of the Czech Revitalization Agency, an experienced international AMC was hired to manage the entity. The AMC may choose to outsource the servicing of the portfolio to the originating bank

[NAMA or SAREB] or other banks (IBRA). However, it can be difficult to fully align incentives, particularly in those cases where the banks themselves are undergoing intensive restructuring programs. In SAREB's case, the banks proved incapable of providing the required information. Outsourcing services should be awarded in an open competitive bidding process and also require high levels of oversight to insure that the servicer is meeting its obligations under the contract.

What is the Role of Consultants?

Consultants (or outside advisers) can be a useful source of advice. Newly established AMCs are operating in uncharted waters while under great pressure to show results quickly. Consultants can help jump-start the process by providing insights on what similar entities have done and how their solutions might be adapted to fit the existing situation. Outside advisers will also be necessary when conducting portfolio sales to ensure that the portfolio is properly priced and marketed. Outside advisers should be hired by an open competitive bidding process; their scope of work and other terms of their contract should be clearly defined; and their output and billing should be monitored carefully to ensure full compliance.

Consultants, however, should not be used as a replacement for staff nor are they a good source of knowledge transfer. Emerging markets frequently lack the necessary skill sets for managing, restructuring, and selling distressed assets. In these cases, management must guard against the expedient solution of relying heavily on outside expertise and ensure that their recommendations are appropriate and implementable, rather than merely designed to sell product. Outside advisers are project oriented and thus not good sources of knowledge transfer. The international financial institutions and bilateral donors have all provided significant amounts of assistance to build capacity within AMCs. IBRA's overreliance on consultants seriously damaged its reputation owing to the costs involved and the lack of capacity building within the organization.

Strategic Planning and Asset Management

Why is a Strategic Plan Important?

The strategic plan guides the design and operation of an AMC. This high-level, multiyear plan covers the entire life span of an AMC, outlines the overall direction of the organization, and establishes KPIs. It basically answers the three key questions: What is the AMC going to do? How is it going to do it? And, how is it going to judge its performance? The strategic plan, begun early in the AMC planning process and finalized by management, should be adopted by the board at one of its earliest meetings. Once approved, the strategic plan should be broadly shared within the organization itself as well as with the general public and other interested parties, to build support for the AMC and its work. For example, the RTC incorporated the strategic plan for asset disposition into its disposition manual to ensure that all staff understood the methodologies to be employed.

How Often Should the Strategic Plan be Reviewed and Revised?

Strategic plans should be reviewed annually in conjunction with annual business plans and revised only if the underlying fundamentals of the business change. NAMA is required by law to provide information to the minister of finance annually regarding its proposed strategies and policies. Unless the underlying fundamentals of the business change, strategic plans require few, if any, revisions. An example of an appropriate revision is IBRA's shift in strategic direction from restructuring to rapid asset disposition once it became clear that the restructuring strategy would not allow IBRA to meet its mandate.

How Does the Business Plan Differ from the Strategic Plan?

In contrast to the strategic plan, the business plan is prepared on an annual basis and contains a detailed forecast of an AMC's operations. This plan, generally built from the bottom up, includes detailed information on financing needs, financial forecasts, disposition strategies and timing, levels of staffing, and the like. It also sets the targets or goals for collections and shows how the AMC will repay its bonds. Used to monitor the performance of the AMC, it is generally reviewed on a quarterly basis. Significant deviations from the plan require the immediate implementation of corrective actions to ensure that targets are met.

What are Key Performance Indicators?

KPIs are quantifiable measures used to assess an organization's progress in meeting its strategic and operational goals. They are critical to show that the AMC is serious about meeting its objectives. Although KPIs have varied among AMCs, depending on their mandates and circumstances, the two most widely used have been speed of asset disposition and percentage of asset recovery. Other examples include progress on restructuring the debt of the largest borrowers (IBRA); recoveries from bank owners (IBRA and SDIF); proceeds from collections (both gross and net of expenses), and bond redemptions (NAMA). As KPIs provide an early warning signal of performance problems, they should be reviewed by management frequently and corrective action plans implemented in a timely manner.

How Does an AMC Effectively Recover Distressed Assets?

AMCs have a mix of recovery strategies available to them. Table 3.2 provides a snapshot of the most common recovery strategies and the assets for which they are most appropriate. Successful AMCs mix and match recovery strategies depending on the nature of the assets managed, the urgency of cash generation, and their life span. For instance, when an AMC starts operating, it will likely enter into quick-recovery programs with small borrowers in order to generate cash and show early progress in recovery. These programs have been controversial in that they involve a discount from book value for the quick payment of the loan. If the authorities do not wish to be seen to be granting discounts, the portfolios should be sold. Sales of smaller NPL portfolios are also likely in the near term, to generate cash as well as get an early test of investor appetite. Although restructuring is predicated on receiving a higher recovery on a performing loan, it takes time and—as in IBRA's case—may not be feasible when large numbers of loans need restructuring; restructuring skills are not readily available; or the enforcement and insolvency regimes are weak. In such cases, a rapid disposition program of transparent, open loan sales is preferable even though they run the risk of allowing borrowers to repurchase their loans at a discount.

Although quick-recovery programs and NPL sales result in the immediate reduction of assets under management, loan administration and restructuring is a continuing process (figure 3.1). Assets must be actively managed as long as they remain on the books of an AMC. This means not only that the borrowers need to receive regular statements of their accounts but also that every effort be made to return the account to a current status. Even AMCs with the narrowest of mandates—rapid asset disposition—will need to engage in these activities either directly or by outsourcing the functions to an asset manager. To be effective, the process must begin with a thorough assessment of a borrower's ability to repay. Enforcement actions or insolvency proceedings should begin immediately for those borrowers who lack repayment capacity or are uncooperative. Loan restructuring is appropriate only when borrowers are cooperative and have the ability to repay their obligations (that is, viable, as in the case of the advanced real estate management strategies used by NAMA and SAREB).[2]

Figure 3.1 Loan Restructuring Process

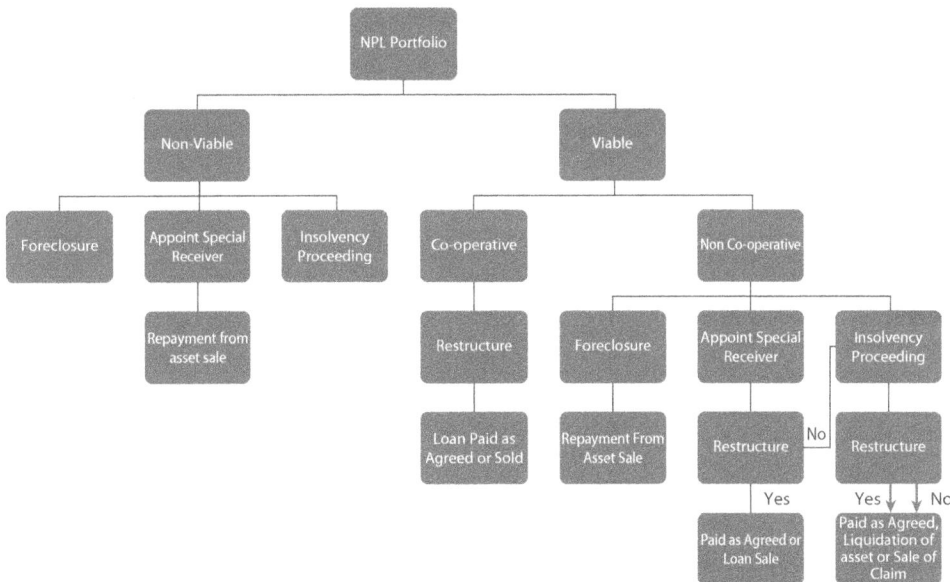

Source: World Bank.

The term "loan restructuring" should not be confused with "corporate restructuring." Neither process requires that the firm be preserved or left intact. Indeed, most "loan restructuring" plans contain one or more of the following elements: the liquidation or sale of some or all of the company's assets to a third party; removal and replacement of some or all of the corporation's ownership or management; and, in many cases, a compromise of the debt owed to creditors. The essential difference between the two approaches is that in the case of loan restructuring, the AMC works with the borrower to develop a repayment plan and continues to hold a loan, while "corporate restructuring" requires that the owners are removed and the AMC (as owner) drives the process either directly (Securum) or through special administrators (Danaharta) with the AMC's ultimate recovery coming from the sale of its equity in the entity.

Thus, corporate restructuring is not necessarily appropriate for all AMCs. Danaharta had special powers to perform corporate restructuring and appointed 73 special administrators. Average recoveries with this method were similar to those for foreclosure and were much lower than the ones for plain loan /financial restructuring (table 3.1). There may be specific job considerations that call for an AMC to embark on corporate restructuring, but if an AMC does not have the required human resources, this task is more appropriately outsourced.

What is an Out-of-Court Restructuring Framework and Who Needs One?

A consensual approach to loan restructuring is preferable. An approach in which the borrower and creditors agree without resorting to a legal process is preferable as it saves money and time, both of which are better spent rehabilitating the borrower. In the early 1970s the Bank of England developed a methodology to guide

Table 3.1 Danaharta: Recovery Rates from Various Recovery Methods, September 2005

Recovery method	Adjusted LRA RM billion (a)		Recovery RM billion (b)		Recovery rate (%) (c)=(b)/(a)	
	Acquired NPLs	Managed NPLs	Acquired NPLs	Managed NPLs	Acquired NPLs	Managed NPLs
Plain loan restructuring	1.07	3.77	0.86	3.58	80	95
Settlement	3.55	8.55	3.11	6.41	88	75
Schemes of arrangement	3.14	6.82	1.84	4.32	59	63
Appointments of Special Administrators	1.66	2.59	0.84	0.58	51	22
Foreclosure	9.12	3.69	2.62	1.65	29	45
Others	3.81	3.29	1.74	2.6	46	79
Legal Action	0.28	1.08	0.06	0.14	20	13
Total	**22.63**	**29.79**	**11.07**	**19.28**	**49**	**65**
Overall		52.42		30.35		58

LRA = Loan right acquired, which includes the original transfer value of the loan and interest accrued from the date of acquisition
Source: Danaharta (2005).
Note: NPLs = nonperforming loan.

such restructurings. Now known as the "London Approach," it basically provides a set of rules to be followed by both parties during the negotiation process. In its simplest format, it calls for a short payment moratorium to allow the banks time to determine whether a restructuring is feasible. During this "standstill" period, the borrower agrees to provide all requested financial information to support a restructuring and agrees to not undertake any action that is unfavorable to the banks. The banks, in return, agree not to pursue legal actions. If a restructuring is not possible, both parties are free to pursue legal actions. Although the Bank of England brokered the agreements in the beginning, it gradually reduced its role and the process ultimately became the standard practice for undertaking a loan restructuring in developed countries. In emerging markets, where banks are unfamiliar with the restructuring process and the insolvency system supports liquidation rather than rehabilitation, the Asian countries and Turkey found it helpful to institute these framework agreements. They were based on the London Approach and were used to facilitate a more timely and efficient restructuring process. Figure 3.2 provides a simplified illustration of the process.

Figure 3.2 Out-of-Court Restructuring Framework

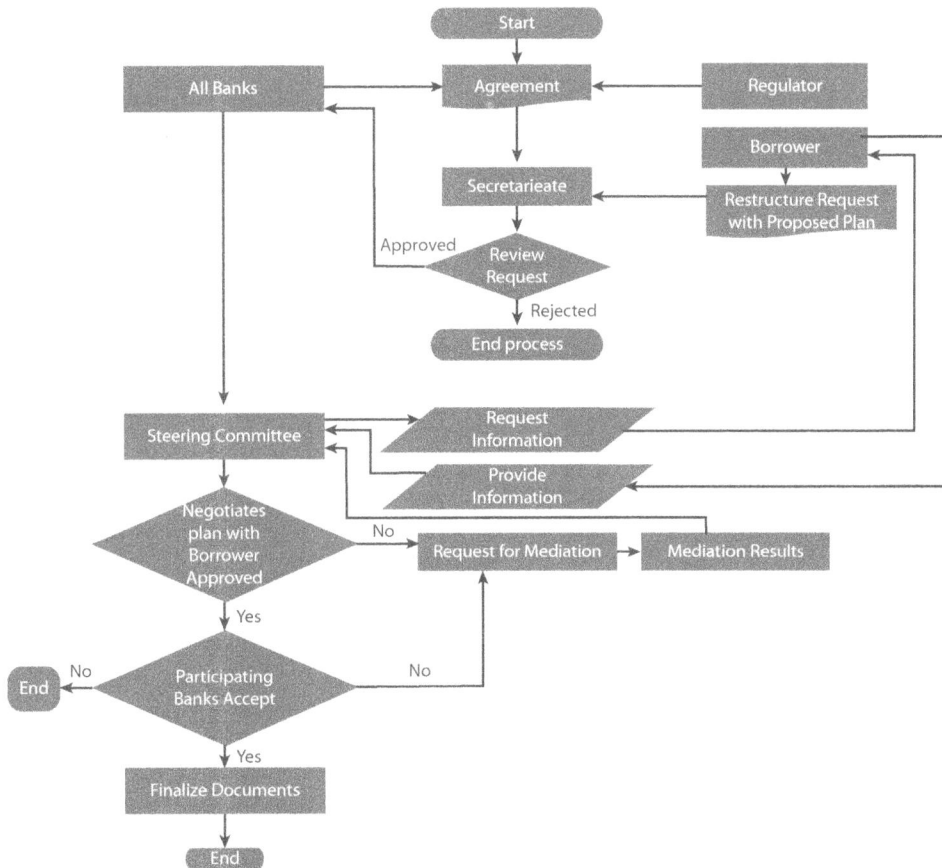

Source: World Bank.

Public Asset Management Companies • http://dx.doi.org/10.1596/978-1-4648-0874-6

Table 3.2 Recovery Strategies by Loan Type

Recovery Strategies	Description	Pros	Cons	Appropriate for			
				Consumer	SMEs	Corporate	Real Estate
Quick-Recovery Programs	Select group of borrowers targeted through a specialized, focused effort requiring additional resources, specialized approach, and high managerial focus	Early cash recoveries Incentivizes debtors to perform Requires willingness to grant discounts	Requires strong internal push and resources to accomplish results Resolves a large number of low-value accounts quickly Possible moral hazard issues	X	X		
NPL Sales	Selected portfolios or individual loans marketed to maximize sales opportunities	Cash recoveries Permanent solution Reduces funding and staffing needs	May result in borrowers buying back loans at discount	X	X	X	X
Traditional Restructuring	Revision of loan terms, contractual agreements, collateral coverage, and the like	Returns entities to profitability Maintains companies and employment	Lengthy process Requires high staff levels May be cosmetic rather than lasting solution		X	X	X
Advanced Real Estate Management	Requires establishing a specialized company to (i) repossess, (ii) manage, and (iii) sell real estate properties	Maintains or increases asset value Restarts real estate market Enhances professionalism and standards	Long time frame and costly Requires specialized skills Requires funding project development and possible finance of property sales				X

table continues next page

Table 3.2 Recovery Strategies by Loan Type *(continued)*

Recovery Strategies	Description	Pros	Cons	Appropriate for			
				Consumer	SMEs	Corporate	Real Estate
Enforcement	Should be promptly entered into whenever borrower is uncooperative or collateral value exceeds borrower's repayment ability	Helps to restore credit discipline Starts the clock on the recovery process	Lengthy process Cost of proceeding may reduce recovery proceeds	X	X	X	X
Debt-to-Equity Swaps	Requires establishing dedicated vehicle to acquire equity shares held by the AMC	Possible value creation through opportunistic transactions Platform open to external investors, which may reduce risk for the AMC	Requires deep, liquid equity markets Borrowers must be likely candidates for future equity offering Requires specialized skills Not suitable for most emerging markets			X	X

Note: AMC = asset management company; NPL = nonperforming loan.

To work effectively, these regimes must work "in the shadow of the law." Borrowers who fail to perform must be subjected to insolvency proceedings, in which their treatment is likely to be harsher. And they require a legal mechanism to bind dissenting creditors. On balance, these regimes have been useful in providing interim restructuring and stabilization for a large number of borrowers within a relatively short period of time. But several rounds of restructuring were required before a permanent solution was reached. They were less effective when AMCs with special powers participated in the process. Many foreign banks refused to participate in both Indonesia and Turkey, as they feared the AMC's special powers would place them at a disadvantage. Local banks in Turkey also complained that they had to bear a disproportionate share of the losses as the SDIF was precluded by law from granting debt forgiveness. And they proved ineffective at binding dissenting creditors to a plan. As a result, many jurisdictions have moved to enact legislation that provides an expedited process, known as a "prepackaged bankruptcy," to enable the courts to approve a plan that has already been approved by a majority of creditors.

Internal Controls and Transparency

Why are Internal Controls Important?

Internal controls ensure that the agency is in material compliance with all laws and regulations, assets are safeguarded against material loss, and financial statements are reliable. AMCs, with their rapidly expanding workload, staffing, and mandates, face particular challenges with respect to internal controls. It is easy to dismiss as unnecessarily burdensome such basic control elements as segregation of duties, accuracy cross-checks, and authorization and verification procedures. However, loss of control has the potential to become a crisis of its own and can easily destroy the credibility of and support for the organization. In the spring of 1990, the RTC quickly resolved 155 failed thrifts in 31 states, without adequate controls to ensure that the assets were properly reflected in the RTC's system. It was subsequently discovered that the records and ledger of the Western Region were out of balance by some US$7 billion. The problem received extensive press coverage and criticism, cost US$25 million to correct, and revealed major weaknesses in the RTC's contracting process.

Internal controls need to be fully integrated into an internal review risk-based framework. In addition to traditional internal review processes, the framework should include a formalized process that identifies management accountability at all levels in the organization and ties the control of risk to program objectives; holds senior management responsible for managing weaknesses in internal controls; and creates and maintains an independent management reporting system of identified weaknesses, including the implementation and tracking of corrective action plans.

What Is the Role of Information Systems?

The board and management require reliable and timely information about all of an AMC's resolution efforts (NPLs and banks, if included in the mandate). The first and foremost operational step is to collect the data on assets and borrowers and input the data properly into an information system that is designed to meet the AMC's mission and business strategy. This system must be able to accurately identify assets and target them for specific disposition programs, provide the information necessary to evaluate the performance of these efforts, enable proper oversight and management of outside asset-servicing providers (if used), and track progress on meeting the AMC's objectives across all its resolution activities.

Large, complex, proprietary information systems take time to develop and implement. At NAMA, starting from an Excel spreadsheet, it took two and a half years to implement a fully developed information system. SAREB was able to complete the process in the record time of one and a half years.

Are the Transparency Requirements Outlined in the Law Sufficient?

An AMC should strive to exceed the requirements contained in its enabling legislation with respect to transparency. As public entities with a commercial focus, AMCs must go beyond the usual standards of preserving the public's right to access documents and attend proceedings to allow for effective oversight. They must embrace a more commercial approach that requires the full, accurate, and timely disclosure of relevant information. Danaharta, SDIF, KAMCO, NAMA, and SAREB have all excelled in this regard; by contrast, information on Asset Management Corporation of Nigeria (AMCON's) performance is not readily available.

What are the Benefits of Increased Transparency?

Transparency allows an AMC to build and maintain support for its work. Transparency extends beyond the mere release of information. It also applies to how an AMC conducts itself in its dealings internally with staff as well as externally with borrowers, investors, vendors, and the general public. Organizations generate trust and respect by conducting themselves in an honest and open manner; creating a work environment that encourages problem identification and prompt implementation of corrective action plans; anticipating the public's questions and concerns; and making management available to meet with relevant stakeholders. In contrast, those that are reluctant to disclose more than the bare minimum of information; that fail to provide the rationale for changes in policy or direction; that become defensive when questions are raised about operations, or that have consistent unexplained budget overruns are felt to be hiding something and quickly lose public support.

How can Transparency and a Culture of Openness be Fully Integrated into Daily Operations?

The design and maintenance of a website is an integral part of a transparency program. The website content should include all the financial and operational documents, such as management testimony to the legislature or other oversight bodies; financial plans and results; newspaper articles; key policies, including a code of conduct for dealing with borrowers; the enabling legislation as well as the strategic plan; and notices regarding asset sales. NAMA's website (https://www.nama.ie) provides an excellent example of a website that promotes transparency.

Codes of conduct and a more open restructuring process have also proved useful. AMCs have long been subject to codes of conduct regarding confidentiality, conflicts of interest, insider dealing, market manipulation, prohibition of discrimination, and disclosure of personal interest. These are provided by corporate law (for Securum and Danaharta) or by government regulation. With the evolution of more commercially focused AMCs, these codes are now posted on their websites as well as contained in their internal policy manuals. The introduction of corporate restructuring frameworks in East Asia and Turkey based on the London Approach also provided borrowers with badly needed information on the restructuring process as well as provided clear-cut "rules of the game." NAMA, in particular, has set new standards for open disclosure with the expansion of codes of practice to a number of nontraditional areas (disposal of bank assets, risk management, and servicing standards for loan portfolios). And they have also developed a standardized format to be used by all borrowers when submitting resolution proposals to the agency.

Closing the AMC

How is an AMC Closed and When Should the Process Begin?

An AMC generally begins the windup process as assets are disposed of. As the size of the NPL portfolio shrinks, AMCs begin to reduce their size through the closure of regional operations (the RTC), the consolidation of AMCs with small amounts of residual assets (Securum and Retriva), and staff redundancies (NAMA).

The transfer of an AMC's assets requires careful planning that needs to begin well in advance of its termination date. An AMC's enabling legislation should designate how residual assets are to be handled, either through designating a specific institution (the Federal Deposit Insurance Corporation (FDIC) in the case of the RTC) or the ministry empowered to make the decision (usually the Ministry of Finance). Good practice would suggest a process similar to that followed by the RTC. Approximately one year before the termination date, a task force, composed of representatives from both the RTC and the FDIC, was created to develop and implement the transfer process. Appropriate internal controls were put in place within both organizations to ensure that the transfer of the RTC's assets, personnel, and operations was accomplished efficiently without financial loss, delays in completing the AMC's remaining work, or loss of public confidence. Once the assets have been transferred, the closing process would follow established practices for the windup of commercial or public agencies.

An AMC should prepare and publish a comprehensive record of its activities. It is important to leave a detailed record of how and what was done, so that it is available to guide future actions, should any be needed, and to provide advice to others facing similar situations. All of the now-closed AMCs produced a study or analysis of their experiences. However, with the passage of time, many have been lost. The experiences of the RTC and the SDIF have remained readily available as they were either part of or closely associated with permanent deposit insurance agencies. For more-temporary agencies, consideration should be given to maintaining access to these records on the website of a permanent agency such as the bank supervisor agency, central bank, or Ministry of Finance.

How Should an AMC's Performance Be Assessed?

An AMC's performance should be assessed by how well it fulfilled its initial mandate and how much it contributed to reducing the cost of the crisis. Whereas early AMCs were assessed largely against their recovery rates (gross basis), with the evolution to more commercial entities the focus has shifted to take into account the overall contribution of the AMC to reducing the cost of the crisis (net basis). Thus, in addition to assessing how well the AMC fulfilled its mandate, today's focus is on the ability of the AMC to repay its bonds, thereby reducing the government's contingent liability with respect to the cost of the crisis. For the purposes of this toolkit, AMCs are considered successful when they repay the interest and principal of their bonds. Initial capital is seldom repaid and represents the government's fixed cost of the crisis. Table 3.3 provide a snapshot of the characteristics and performance of the AMCs studies in this paper.

Notes

1. This committee was abolished upon the sale of the Northern Ireland portfolio.
2. It is interesting to note that NAMA does not own any real estate assets. Instead, it has chosen a strategy of working out repayment plans with cooperative borrowers and with special administrators and receivers when borrowers are uncooperative.

Table 3.3 Key Characteristics of AMCs

a. Legal and Institutional Structure

AMC	Early AMCs			Asian Crisis and Aftermath			Current AMCs		
	RTC	Securum	KAMCO	IBRA	Danaharta	SDIF	NAMA	AMCON	SAREB
Country	United States	Sweden	Korea, Rep. of	Indonesia	Malaysia	Turkey	Ireland	Nigeria	Spain
Date Established	1989	1993	1997	1998	1998	1999	2009	2010	2012
Legal Basis	Law	Companies Act	Law	Presidential Decree and Banking Law	Companies Act	Banking Law	Law	Law	Law
Ownership	State	State	47.2% private, 42.8% state	State	State	State	51% private, 49% state	State	Private
Official Mandate	Resolve thrifts (banks)	Restructure NPLs of state-owned Nordenbanken, later expanded to include Gota	Purchase, manage, and dispose of NPLs	Resolve banks, administer deposit guarantee, and recover misused liquidity support	Purchase, manage, and dispose of NPLs; receiver of two failed banks	Resolve banks, administer deposit guarantee, and recover misused liquidity support	Purchase, manage and dispose of NPLs	Purchase, manage and dispose of NPLs, recapitalize failed banks, and invest in equities	Purchase, manage, and dispose of NPLs
Special Powers	None	None	None	Right to transfer assets without borrower's permission; examine borrowers' shareholders and key bank personnel; freeze assets; seize debtor's assets through special administrative process; review and terminate contracts	Acquire assets through vesting; appoint special administrator; sell assets by private treaty	Make shareholders explicitly liable for misuse of liquidity support; assets designated as "State Receivables" providing power to seize and sell debtor's assets regardless of whether they had been pledged	Use vesting orders and compulsory purchase orders; receive information from tax authorities and protection against claims if payment received from insolvent borrowers; appoint special administrator	Appoint special administrator; special powers in bankruptcy and winding-up proceedings	None
Life span	Seven years	None specified, 10–15 years envisioned; reduced to five	None specified	Six years	Seven years	None specified	Anticipated to be 15 years	None specified	15 years

table continues next page

Table 3.3 Key Characteristics of AMCs *(continued)*
b. Asset Transfer Mechanism

AMC	Early AMCs			Asian Crisis & Aftermath			Current AMCs		
	RTC	Securum	KAMCO	IBRA	Danaharta	SDIF	NAMA	AMCON	SAREB
Country	United States	Sweden	Korea, Rep. of	Indonesia	Malaysia	Turkey	Ireland	Nigeria	Spain
Methodology	n.a. (did not purchase assets)	n.a. (did not purchase assets)	Internal pricing based on present value of cash flows	n.a. (did not purchase assets)	Real estate: market value based on new appraisal; equity: market value; unsecured: 10% of outstanding principal	n.a. (did not purchase assets)	Discounted cash flow plus uplift factor of 8.3% on average, reflecting improvement in real estate market over time	Guidelines issued by central bank	Transfer price determined by BoS based on independent valuation reports (AQR)
Discount from book value	n.a.	n.a.	64%	n.a.	54%	n.a.	57%	54%	52.4%
Participation	n.a.	n.a.	Voluntary	n.a.	Voluntary (mandatory if public recapitalization)	n.a.	Voluntary	Voluntary	Mandatory for public recapitalization
Incentives	n.a.	n.a.	0% risk weight on bonds; minimum CAR increased to 8%	n.a.	Losses amortized up to five years; 0% risk weight on bonds; profit sharing of 80% of surplus ≥ purchase price and costs	n.a.	None	NPLs not to exceed 5% of total loans	Participation in SAREB linked to public recapitalization
Eligible Loans	n.a.	n.a.	Loans classified substandard and below whose security and transfer were legally executable; priority for NPLs whose removal was critical to restructuring originating institutions as well as NPLs with multiple creditors	n.a.	Large and industrial loans above RM 5 million	n.a.	Large real estate loans together with any related loans to borrower	Any loan reasonably expected to become substandard within three months or to result in loss of at least 1% of assets within six months; no criteria for equity purchases	NPLs with net book value ≥ €250,000, foreclosed properties with net book value ≥ €100,000, and other loans and properties originating from RE borrowers over which bank had control

table continues next page

Table 3.3 Key Characteristics of AMCs (continued)

c. Performance

	Early AMCs			Asian Crisis & Aftermath			Current AMCs		
AMC	RTC	Securum	KAMCO	IBRA	Danaharta	SDIF	NAMA	AMCON	SAREB
Country	United States	Sweden	Korea, Rep. of	Indonesia	Malaysia	Turkey	Ireland	Nigeria	Spain
Funding									
Government Bonds	$30.1 billion		Won 20.5 trillion	Recapitalization bonds issued directly by government.	RM 11 billion		€30.2 billion	₦3.5 trillion	€50.8 billion
Budget	$60.0 billion	Skr 24 billion	Won 0.5 billion	Annual recovery targets established and proceeds net of expenses remitted to reduce budget deficit	RM 3 billion	$17 billion		₦10 billion	€1.2 billion
Banks	$1.2 billion					$2 billion		Banking Sector Resolution Fund (per year: central bank, ₦50 billion; banks, 0.5% of assets)	
Central Bank									
Insurance Premiums						Minor amount			
Sub Debt			Won 0.5 trillion				€1.6 billion		€3.6 billion
Total	$91.3 billion	Skr 24 billion	Won 21.5 trillion		RM 14 billion	$19 billion	€31.8 billion		€55.6 billion
Repayment to Treasury	$395 billion[a]	Skr 14 billion	n.a.	Rp 151 trillion (all recoveries)	RM 13 billion	$6.5 billion plus $2 billion to central bank	~€16 billion	n.a.	n.a.
Assets Remaining at termination	3%	2%	40%	40% of NPLs	3.6% (RM 1.72 billion)	n.a.	n.a.	n.a.	n.a.
Recovery Rate (Face Value)	87% (on assets only)	n.a.	46.8%	22% (NPL only)	58%	16% (NPL sales only)	~33% (end 2014)	n.a.	n.a.

Note: AMC = asset management company; NPL = nonperforming loan; SAREB = Sociedad de Gestión de Activos Procedentes de la Reestructuración Bancaria (Spain); AMCON = Asset Management Corporation of Nigeria; RTC = Resolution Trust Corporation (United States); KAMCO = Korea Asset Management Corporation (Korea); IBRA = Indonesian Bank Restructuring Agency (Indonesia); SDIF = Savings Deposit Insurance Fund (Turkey); NAMA = National Asset Management Agency (Ireland).

[a]. This amount represents the gross cash proceeds received from asset disposition activities. The total cost of resolving the S&Ls (depositor payoffs and settlement of liabilities and claims) exceeded this amount by some $88 billion. Of the $91 billion provided, all but $3.4 billion was required to absorb the permanent losses embedded in these institutions. Of all AMCs surveyed, the RTC is the only one that fully absorbed the losses of the banking crisis; more recently, AMCON absorbed the negative equity of failed banks, though its deficit is intended to be offset over time by a Banking Sector Resolution Fund funded by annual contributions from the central bank and commercial banks. In all other cases, the costs of resolving the banks were borne directly by the government.

PART II

Case Studies: Three Generations of Public AMCs

CHAPTER 4

The First Generation: The RTC and Securum

The RTC, United States

Context of the Creation of the RTC

The 1980s through the mid-1990s saw an unprecedented number of financial institutions fail in the United States. During that period, 2,912 institutions failed, of which 1,295 (44 percent) were thrifts (savings and loan associations) insured by the Federal Savings and Loan Insurance Corporation (FSLIC).[1] Together these institutions accounted for some US$621 billion in assets (11 percent of gross domestic product, or GDP), resulting in the need to resolve, on average, some US$113 million of assets each day over the 15-year period. The workload was not evenly distributed over the period, with the bulk of the thrift failures (927 institutions or 72 percent) occurring between 1989 and 1992.

The roots of the thrift crisis lay in the nature of these institutions. Relatively small in size and local in nature, the thrift industry provided the preponderance of residential mortgage lending in the United States. With the interest rate paid on deposits regulated and few alternative investments for the small retail customer, these institutions relied on relatively low-cost deposits to fund their long-term, fixed-rate mortgage loans. Beginning in the late 1970s, interest rates rose dramatically,[2] deposit funding dried up, as customers flocked to the newly created money market funds that paid market rates and the mark-to-market value of the S&L mortgage portfolios[3] plummeted, resulting by mid-1982 in a combined negative net worth of all S&Ls of US$100 billion.

In the face of intense political pressure, rather than confronting the problem directly, the regulatory and legislative response was aimed at postponing loss recognition and granting expanded powers to the industry in hopes that it would grow out of its problems. The Depository Institutions Deregulation and Monetary Control Act of 1980 phased out interest rate ceilings for deposits, broadened the powers of thrift institutions, and raised the deposit insurance limit from US$40,000 to US$100,000. Two years later, the Garn–St. Germain Depository Institutions Act of 1982 (i) allowed banks and thrifts to issue money market deposit accounts to stem disintermediation; (ii) authorized a program of temporary forbearance through the use of net worth certificates[4] to buy time for thrifts to correct interest rate imbalances and restore capital levels; and (iii) increased the authority of thrifts to invest in commercial loans so as to strengthen the institution's viability over the long term. This legislation set the stage for a rapid expansion of lending, unwarranted risk taking, an increase in competition between thrifts and banks, overbuilding, and the subsequent collapse of the commercial real estate market.

In addition to the severe financial stress resulting from the changes in the financial marketplace, the industry also suffered from four severe regional and sectoral recessions: the collapse of farm prices in the Midwest; the decline in oil prices in 1981 and again in 1985 in Texas and other energy-producing states; the decline in defense spending in California during the general recessions of 1989 and 1992; and the collapse of real estate activity and prices in the northeast. Approximately 78 percent of bank failures occurred in these four regions.

By early 1989, the FSLIC, faced with some 600 seriously troubled thrift institutions, had exhausted its reserves and its insurance fund was insolvent. Congress responded by passing the Financial Institutions Reform, Recovery, and Enforcement Act (FIRREA), which abolished the Federal Savings and Loan Insurance Corporation and the Federal Home Loan Bank Board, authorized the use of taxpayer funds to resolve failed thrifts, and created the RTC.

Mandate and Legal Powers

The RTC was established as a thrift resolution entity, not strictly as an asset management entity. Under the FIRREA, the RTC's initial mandate was to merge or liquidate savings associations previously insured by the FSLIC that would be declared insolvent during the period between January 1, 1989, and August 8, 1992. This meant that the RTC had to absorb the losses of the thrifts, if assets were not sufficient to pay or transfer protected deposits. It did not purchase assets from open financial institutions like several of the AMCs featured in this report. It was responsible for the resolution of failed financial institutions that had been placed in conservatorship and receivership. This resulted in the AMC managing rather than owning the assets of these institutions, thus eliminating issues regarding the transfer price of the assets, incentives for participation, or types of assets eligible for transfer. Three main objectives were defined:

- Maximize the net present value return from the disposition of failed thrifts and their assets
- Minimize the effect of these transactions on the local real estate market
- Maximize the affordability and availability of residential real property for low- and moderate-income purchasers

The RTC had a sunset clause but no special powers. The FIRREA contained a sunset clause of December 1996, which was accelerated to December 1995 by the RTC Completion Act in 1993. It did not have special powers to override the foreclosure and insolvency laws.

The RTC had to reach efficiency targets, while also being given a social mandate. The FIRREA mandated that it hire private sector contractors for the disposition of assets whenever available, practical, and efficient. It established a minimum disposition price for assets of not less than 90 percent of market (appraised) value. The RTC Completion Act required the RTC to adopt a number of management reforms; provide business opportunities to minorities and women when issuing management contracts or selling assets; and support affordable housing.[5]

The RTC was initially established under the oversight of the Federal Deposit Insurance Corporation (FDIC), with a separate board. In the FIRREA, the FDIC was named as manager of the RTC and made responsible for appointing the chief executive officer (CEO). Another act in 1991 separated the FDIC and the RTC, with the CEO now being appointed by the president and confirmed by the Senate. In addition, the RTC Oversight Board was established. Its membership consisted of the secretary of the treasury, who served as chairman; the chairman of the Federal Reserve Board; the secretary of housing and urban development; and two private sector representatives appointed by the president. In addition to appointing the president and CEO to manage the RTC, the board's role, working with the RTC and the FDIC, was to develop and establish strategies and policies to govern the RTC's work.

Establishment and Early Years

Headquartered in Washington, D.C., the RTC opened regional offices in Atlanta, Dallas, Denver, and Kansas City and established 14 consolidated offices and 14 sales centers. Initially staffed with employees seconded from the FDIC, the RTC hired additional employees from the private sector and reached a peak staffing level of 8,614 employees in 1991. During its lifetime, the RTC assumed responsibility for and resolved 747 thrifts with assets of US$402.6 billion. These institutions were primarily resolved by the use of purchase and assumption transactions for the sale of both institutions as well as branches (67 percent). Resolution through straight deposit payoffs was used in only 12 percent of the cases (table 4.1).

Table 4.1 RTC Resolution Methods, 1989–95

	Total	
Method	Number	Percent
Branch-insured deposit transfer	34	4
Straight deposit payoff	92	12
Branch purchase and assumption	119	16
Insured deposit transfer	124	17
Standard purchase and assumption	378	51
Total	**747**	**100**

Source: RTC, Statistical Abstract, August 1989/September 1995, pp. 56–57.
Note: RTC = Resolution Trust Corporation (United States).

Primary emphasis was placed on the use of purchase and assumption transactions to resolve failed thrifts. This was largely the result of the FDIC having initially managed the RTC and the RTC staff (largely seconded from the FDIC) continuing to follow the familiar FDIC statutory policies and procedures. Several features, however, evolved over time due to differences between the two organizations and their mandates:

- The RTC made greater use of conservatorships than the FDIC. In part this was dictated by the RTC's lack of sufficient internal resources to fund prompt resolutions. Upon failure, thrifts were passed through a receiver to a newly chartered federal mutual association, the conservatorship. While under the control and oversight of the RTC, the institution's condition was evaluated and the most cost-effective resolution method determined while simultaneously minimizing losses, limiting growth by curtailing new lending, and reducing deposits by lowering above-market rates at maturity, eliminating speculative activities, and terminating any insider waste, fraud, or abuse.
- As the identity of banks placed in conservatorships was known, the RTC's marketing process was more public than that of the FDIC.[6] Bids could be solicited from a wider variety of investors, and information packages contained more detailed information. Over time, the RTC developed standard procedures, legal documents, and forms for use in all resolutions so that potential purchasers had only to acquaint themselves with one set of procedures and documents, regardless of how many institutions they were bidding on.
- The RTC focused on selling assets from the conservatorships or receiverships, selling only a limited number of assets to the acquirer at resolution. Reasons for this included the aforementioned funding difficulties as well as the sheer volume of assets coupled with the relatively lengthy time span (13 months on average) for the conservatorships. Of the US$403 billion in assets assumed by the RTC, only US$75 billion (19 percent) was sold at acquisition. The bulk of the assets, some US$170 billion (42 percent) were sold after the institution's resolution and US$158 billion (39 percent) was sold while the institution was in conservatorship.

Funding

Unlike the FDIC, the RTC had no internal source of funding from insurance premiums. Instead, it was totally reliant on taxpayer funding to cover both permanent losses and working capital. Funding the cost of resolution required separate legislation for each appropriation and was politically divisive. As a result, the numerous funding delays, the longest of which consisted of a 21-month period between March 1992 and December 1993 severely hampered resolution efforts.

In total, Congress authorized three tranches of funding totaling US$105.1 billion of which the RTC utilized US$91.3 billion to fund the losses. Of this amount, US$31.3 billion was raised off budget through 30-year bond offerings totaling US$30.1 billion by a public-private entity called the Resolution Funding Corporation (REFCORP). Taxpayers and the thrift industry would share the burden of paying the interest on these bonds; the principal would be repaid through higher insurance premiums and taxes on the net worth and future prof-its of the industry-owned home loan banks. The Federal Home Loan Banks pro-vided US$1.2 billion, and the balance of the funds were provided by budget appropriations.

Working capital was provided by short-term borrowings from the Federal Financing Bank, secured by the estimated recoveries from asset sales. Loans out-standing under this facility peaked at some US$63 billion during the third quar-ter of 1991 but were subsequently paid in full from the proceeds of asset sales.

Asset Disposition

By the 1990s, the RTC had developed highly sophisticated procedures and strategies to guide the disposition process. Asset portfolios were stratified into pools based on specific criteria such as geographic area, asset type, asset quality, and asset maturity. Then, working closely with the investment community, the RTC tailored products to meet investor needs. Disposition methods included not only the more traditional methods such as regional and national auctions, and large-scale sealed bid and bulk sales, but also more innovative techniques such as securitization and equity partnership arrangements to facilitate the dis-position of harder to sell assets (box 4.1). The RTC also gave representations

---

Box 4.1 Asset Disposition Methods

Auctions: In total, the Resolution Trust Corporation (United States) (RTC) conducted 12 re-gional loan auctions as well as eight national loan auctions. The results of these auctions showed that (i) a certain level of assets was required to make the auction cost-effective; (ii) small regional auctions were as effective as the large national auctions; (iii) reserve pricing was critical as a means to guide market value for the sale of more difficult, complex products; and (iv) reserve pricing was not needed for performing loans as those were easily valued by the bidders.

Real Estate Sales: The RTC conducted real estate sales, including the sale of many pools worth more than US$100 million, through the use of bulk sales as well as sealed bids for the sales of single assets. The process resulted in a faster sale while meeting requirements for broad mar-keting and competitive bidding.

Securitization: Although the RTC was able to dispose of a portion of its portfolio through existing government guarantee programs, the bulk of its mortgage portfolio did not meet the requirements of those agencies. Beginning in December 1990, the RTC began to develop its own securitization program. The loans in this program were of lesser

box continues next page

Box 4.1 Asset Disposition Methods *(continued)*

quality, with such defects as missing documentation, servicing problems, and late payments. Although originally limited to residential mortgages, the program was eventually
expanded to include such "nontraditional" assets as commercial mortgages, multifamily
properties, and consumer loans. The RTC utilized cash reserves and other methods to
provide credit support. More than US$42 billion or 10 percent of its total assets were
resolved through securitization.

Equity Partnerships: Using this method, the RTC sold or contributed assets to a joint venture
between a private sector partner and the RTC. The private sector firm acted as the general
partner and controlled the management and disposition of the assets. The RTC's role was
restricted to having an "equity" interest in the disposition proceeds and arranging financing for the transaction. This method was designed to allow the RTC to obtain a greater
present value recovery from the troubled assets by combining the private sector disposition expertise and efficiencies while providing an opportunity for the RTC to participate in
the upside of the market's recovery from the existing depressed price levels. In total, the
RTC created 72 partnerships with a total asset book value of some US$21 billion. Seven
partnership structures were developed to meet the needs of specific assets and investor
demand.

---

and warranties and provided or facilitated seller financing, which was particularly important in facilitating sales in areas such as the Northeast, which suffered from a severe credit crunch following the 1991–92 recession.

The RTC developed specific strategies to meet its mandate to provide affordable housing for individuals and families. These included providing seller financing for 25 percent of single-family and 33 percent of multifamily properties. It
also developed a program to donate properties with nominal value to a non-
profit organization or public agency, provided that the assets would be used to
for such purposes as homeless shelters, low-income housing, or daycare facilities
for low- and moderate-income families. During its lifetime, the RTC sold
109,141 affordable housing units for a total of more than US$2 billion and
donated more than 1,000 single-family and multifamily assets.

The RTC quickly adopted a strategy of maximizing the use of asset management and disposition contractors. This was based on the FDIC's long experience
with the use of asset management contractors and the RTC's mandate to utilize
the private sector wherever possible. Between 1990 and 1993, the RTC issued
199 Standard Asset Management and Disposition Agreements to 91 contractors,
covering assets with a book value of US$48.5 billion. The contracts covering real
estate and nonperforming loan (NPL)[7] portfolios greater than US$50 million had
an average term of three years and three months, and mandated that the contractor competitively bid and subcontract 12 specific asset management and disposition activities to smaller firms, with particular preference given to minority- and

women-owned businesses. The costs of these subcontractors were reimbursed directly to the contractor by the RTC.

Performance and Winding-up

The RTC successfully met its primary mandates, limiting the total cost of the U.S. thrift crises to 3 percent of GDP. It successfully resolved 747 thrift institutions and disposed of more than US$400 billion of assets, with an average recovery rate of 87 percent. Within asset classes, recovery rates varied widely ranging from 98 percent for the highly liquid cash and investment portfolios to a low of 55 percent for the highly distressed real estate (table 4.2). In addition, it developed programs to provide affordable housing to low- to moderate-income individuals and families and employed the private sector in the disposition process through the use of asset management contracts.

The RTC's high recovery rate was in large part due to the fact that it assumed a portfolio of relatively high-quality assets. Some 77 percent of its assets were in the form of highly liquid cash and investments and mortgages. Eighty percent of the loans it assumed were fully performing and continued to pay according to their contractual terms. Only 20 percent of the loans were classified as nonperforming and slightly less than 7 percent were in the form of distressed real estate.

Lessons Learned

Although the RTC was a resolution company rather than a strict AMC, its experience provides a number of important lessons for those considering the creation of either type of entity:

- Importance of political consensus: From inception, the use of taxpayer funding to cover the costs of resolving the thrifts and their assets was controversial. Much of the discussion revolved around how much, if any, should be included in the current budget periods versus off-budget financing. The continued failure of thrifts, coupled with a lack of reliable estimates of the resolution cost, added to the general unease. While the debate raged, the RTC together with the FDIC, Treasury Department, and Housing and Urban Development

Table 4.2 RTC Recoveries by Asset Type, 1989–95

Asset Type	Share of Total Assets (%)	Recovery (US$ billions)	Share Recovered (%)
Cash and investments	35.6	158	97.8
1–4-Family mortgages	24.7	108	96.1
Other mortgages	16.8	57	75.0
Other loans	7.6	31	88.1
Real estate	6.8	17	55.1
Other assets	8.5	24	62.1
Total	**100.0**	**395**	**86.9**

Source: RTC, Statistical Abstract, August 1989/September 1995, p. 18.
Note: RTC = Resolution Trust Corporation (United States).

Department forged a consensus approach behind the scenes and worked together to ensure the smooth creation, and later the termination, of the entity.
These parties, together with the RTC itself, reached out to the private sector
during both the design phase and the life of the institution to ensure their
support and build confidence in the resolution process.

- Importance of adequate and timely funding: Bank resolution is a costly en-
  deavor requiring both adequate and timely funding. The RTC's periodic lack
  of funding severely hampered its resolution efforts, forcing it to place banks
  in conservatorship for extended periods of time and to place a greater emphasis on selling assets rather than institutions. The lengthy conservatorship period did, however, provide time for the RTC to thoroughly evaluate an institution and its assets, to determine the least-cost approach to resolution, and
  to conduct a more open, transparent bidding process. However, these benefits
  were offset by the increased costs of resolution, as the cost of financing the
  thrifts' assets during conservatorship was higher than the lower government
  borrowing costs of the RTC.

- Early focus on asset disposition: The RTC passed fewer assets to the acquirer
  at the time of purchase than did the FDIC. By the time the assets were offered for sale they were leaner, cleaner institutions unburdened by a large
  legacy of NPLs and in some cases branch networks as well. This, together with
  the funding constraints, forced the RTC to place a greater emphasis on completing asset sales early in the resolution process. An early focus also allowed
  the RTC to quickly place the bulk of the assets, which were performing assets,
  with loan servicers to ensure that borrowers continued to receive their bills
  and make payments, avoiding additional increases in NPLs.

- Use of conservatorships or receiverships avoided transfer pricing issues: By
  dealing only with failed thrifts and using conservator or receiver powers, the
  RTC did not place distressed assets on its balance sheet; instead they remained
  the property of the individual conservatorship or receivership. This avoided
  issues surrounding transfer pricing and allowed the losses upon the disposition of the assets to be reflected where they belonged—on the books of the
  failed thrift. The RTC's role as a recovery agent for already distressed assets
  (as opposed to being seen as the cause of the losses) was thus reinforced in the
  public's mind.

- Speed of asset disposition enhanced by deep liquid capital markets, together
  with a market-driven disposition strategy and asset valuation approach: It is
  clear that the RTC benefited greatly from the deep, liquid U.S. capital market, which allowed it to dispose of a large volume of assets without disrupt-
  ing local real estate prices or relying on individual transactions during a period in which traditional real estate funding sources had dried up. The market
  also allowed the RTC to reach many small retail investors who otherwise
  would have been unable to participate. By working closely with market
  participants, the RTC was able to structure new products (such as equity
  partnerships and securitized commercial mortgages) that met specific needs,

thereby enhancing the disposition process. This new approach was further reinforced by a valuation methodology that valued individual assets from the perspective of an investor. This methodology placed more emphasis on the actual net cash flows produced by the assets, with little reliance on secondary repayment sources such as guarantees. Although this tended to produce lower valuations, the more realistic pricing allowed the RTC to sell assets more quickly.

- The importance of internal controls: Properly designed and implemented internal controls are not visible, nor are their benefits (the lack of mistakes or problems) readily apparent to either staff or the public. The negative results, however, are obvious to all and frequently lead to a loss of confidence in the organization. Based on the basic principles of segregation of duties, checks and balances, and authorizations and verification procedures, these safeguards are frequently dismissed in a rapidly changing, dynamic environment. But it is the relentless and boring adherence to these admittedly basic elements that gives an entity the flexibility to expand and contract, centralize or decentralize operations, and meet evolving strategic objectives without losing control.

- Careful design of incentives and intensive oversight of asset management and disposition contractors: The RTC, faced with an unprecedented growth in assets and a mandate to employ the private sector wherever practical, made extensive use of loan servicing firms and asset management and disposition contractors. Although the benefits were many, including limiting the growth of RTC staff levels and enhancing the speed of disposition, weaknesses were also uncovered. Incentives, particularly with respect to the speed and types of assets to be disposed of, need to be carefully designed to ensure that they are aligned with the strategic goals of the resolution entity. Contract management requires intensive oversight to ensure that the terms of the contract and all policies and procedures are being adhered to. This requires specialized skills not generally found in resolution entities. In the case of the RTC, many of the firms employed were start-ups and required intensive training in asset disposition practices as well as the RTC procedures.

Public Asset Management Companies • http://dx.doi.org/10.1596/978-1-4648-0874-6

Securum, Sweden

Context of the Creation of Securum

The Swedish financial crisis of 1990 through 1993 was a result of a multitude of policy choices by the Swedish authorities over a longer period of time. At the root of the problem was an apparent lack of coordination between tax reform, credit, and foreign exchange market deregulation and monetary policy decisions:

- Credit markets were liberalized rapidly, resulting in a credit boom.
- A tax regime favoring debt, including the step-up of mortgage interest tax deductibility, was unwound and a separate capital gains regime was introduced in the midst of the crisis.
- Foreign exchange controls were removed over a short period of time, with a fixed currency regime in place.
- Restrictive monetary policy, designed to defend the krona in the fixed-rate regime, resulted in extreme hikes in the interest rate and consequent defaults.

Sweden maintained a fixed currency regime from 1977 through November 1992. It was first tied to a trade-weighted currency basket (1977–91) and then to the European Currency Unit (ECU) (1991–92). During the fixed exchange rate regime, Sweden devalued its currency five times, resulting in a devaluation of 45 percent from peak to trough.

The Swedish banking market was strictly regulated until the relatively rapid credit and foreign exchange market deregulation during the second half of the 1980s. In 1983 liquidity quotas for banks were abolished, and in 1985 caps for interest rates and limits to credit growth for banks were eliminated. This led to the growth of an unregulated shadow banking system in the form of finance companies. These firms relied heavily on the banking system for funding, to serve primarily commercial real estate markets and private consumption.

The deregulation of the credit market led to credit expansion of 15 to 20 percent annually, with total lending volume more than doubling from 1986 to 1989. Between 1985 and 1990 the price index for residential real estate and commercial properties more than doubled, as a consequence of both banks and finance companies competing for market share in the now fully deregulated credit market. With the restrictions on bank lending removed and a tax regime favorable for borrowing, companies and households were incentivized to increase their indebtedness. With generous tax deductions for interest payments, the cost of credit was extremely low, at times even negative.

Weaknesses in regulation and supervision as well as banks' own internal risk management practices failed to identify the undue concentration of lending to the real estate sector. It was ultimately discovered that approximately two-thirds of all bank loan exposures were linked to the real estate and commercial property sectors, including loans to developers and real estate management companies, land loans, and loans for commercial purposes secured by real estate.

Public Asset Management Companies • http://dx.doi.org/10.1596/978-1-4648-0874-6

As the final step of deregulation, the remaining foreign exchange controls were removed in 1989. At the same time, Sweden undertook fundamental changes in tax policies, introducing a 30 percent capital gains tax at the time when foreign exchange regulations were lifted. Also noteworthy was the stepped-up reduction of mortgage interest tax deductibility at the height of the crisis. These actions put significant downward pressure on the overheated domestic real estate markets, pushing down prices over a very short period of time.

At the same time, the Swedish economy began to weaken. Industrial production declined and real estate prices fell. In 1990 a number of finance companies experienced significant losses, and in September a large finance company suspended its payments, resulting in the collapse of the commercial paper market. The consequent substantial rise in interest rates led to a crash in already pressured real estate prices, causing collateral values to collapse. Borrowers reacted by selling their collateral, which further contributed to falling prices. Business liquidations and bankruptcies followed in quick succession.

By the end of 1990, reported credit losses in the banking system had increased to about 1 percent of lending, two to three times as much as during earlier years. But this was just the beginning. By the end of 1991, losses were running at 3.5 percent of lending, and at the peak of the crisis in the final quarter of 1992 at 7.5 percent of lending, about twice the operating profits of the banking sector. During 1990–93, accumulated losses came to nearly 17 percent of lending (table 4.3).

A restrictive monetary policy to defend the krona exacerbated the banking crisis. In April 1992, the Central Bank (Riksbank) raised the overnight rates from 16 to 75 percent for a number of days in an effort to defend the krona's tie to the ECU. In mid-September, the Riksbank raised the interest rates to 500 percent over a short period, but speculation against the krona continued. Uncertainty surrounding the monetary policy led to real interest rates rising quite rapidly, from low single digits to double digits, and foreign funding dried up practically overnight. The consequent liquidity crunch and increased costs hit hard the already strained real estate companies and households, driving up

Table 4.3 The Experience of Sweden's Major Banks during the Banking Crisis

	Total Lending, 1985 (SKr Billion)	Increase in Lending, 1985–88 (%)	Total Losses as Share of Lending, 1990–93 (%)
Nordbanken	84.2	78	21.4
Gota	29.8	102	37.3
SEBanken	65.6	76	11.7
Handelsbanken	73.1	38	9.5
Sparbanken Sverige	78.3	88	17.6
Föreningsbanken	23.1	67	16.6
Total		**77**	**16.8**

Source: Wallander 1994.

Public Asset Management Companies • http://dx.doi.org/10.1596/978-1-4648-0874-6

banks' NPLs. The Riksbank was forced to abandon its fixed-rate policy and let the krona float in November 1992. It immediately fell by 20 percent.

Sweden entered the crisis without a systemic resolution framework or a clear regulatory framework for dealing with problem banks. It had no deposit insurance scheme, making crisis management very precarious and sensitive. Relying heavily on lessons learned from the RTC experience and the private sector restructuring of troubled U.S. banks (notably Crocker and Mellon) through the establishment of a "bad bank," and working closely with international consultants, the authorities devised a resolution scheme that relied primarily on private sector solutions, with the state's role limited to leading the restructuring and protecting asset values.

The crisis response consisted of three parts: the issuance of an open-ended guarantee of all banks' liabilities in the autumn of 1992, a bank restructuring program, and the creation of AMCs to recover value from the bad assets. The Bank Support Authority (Bankstödsnämnden) was established under the Ministry of Finance to manage the restructuring process, as it was felt that assigning this responsibility to either the Financial Supervisory Authority or the Riksbank would have diverted their attention from their mandates. The Bankstödsnämnden was responsible for evaluating each bank and for providing government support to those institutions that were viable.

All banks were required to undergo a rigorous examination process to identify the true depth of capital impairment. A Property Valuation Board composed of independent property experts was established to formulate a common methodology and valuation standards to be used by all banks. As a cross-check, approximately 25 percent of the properties were valued on an individual basis by third-party experts.

The Swedish financial crisis affected all Swedish domestic banks. They each ended up resolving their situation very differently, some few independently, others with support from the government (table 4.4). Private banks did not transfer assets to the public AMC, primarily owing to the inability to agree on a transfer price.

Mandate and Legal Powers

Securum constituted a specific part of the overall crisis resolution. It was established as a government-owned finance company to work out the nonperforming assets of state-owned Nordbanken. It began operations on January 1, 1993, with a capitalization of SKr 24 billion (1.4 percent of GDP) to cover its operating costs during the workout period before asset sales began. It received a guarantee from the state to borrow SKr 27 billion from Nordbanken. The majority of the 700 staff came from Nordbanken. The assumed time horizon for working out the impaired assets was 10 to 15 years, and no explicit sunset was stipulated.

Securum was to operate under the Companies Act with no special extraordinary powers or specific legislation, and was deliberately not brought under the

Table 4.4 Crisis Resolution Solution by Bank

Banks	Solution
Handelsbanken and SEB, the largest private commercial banks	Recapitalization by shareholders; establishment of their own bad banks as subsidiaries. No government support beyond benefiting from the blanket guarantee.
Nordesbanken, a majority state-owned bank and third largest	Recapitalization by the state (SKr 14.2 billion in 1991–92) and split between a clean bank and Securum. Government bought out the remaining private shareholders in 1992.
Gota Bank, the fifth largest commercial bank	Taken over and recapitalized by the government in 1993 (SKr 20 billion). Viable parts merged with Nordbanken, and its AMC Retriva merged with Securum.
Första Sparbanken	Merged with 10 other smaller savings banks to form Savings Bank Sverige. Transaction handled within the Saving Bank Group with an initial guarantee and subsequent interest rate subsidies from the government.
Föreninsbanken (cooperative bank)	No state support beyond benefiting from the blanket guarantee and merged eventually with Savings Bank Sverige (later Swedbank).

Note: AMC = asset management company.

supervision of the Financial Supervisory Authority. Extraordinary powers were deemed unnecessary given the existence of adequate bankruptcy and foreclosure legislation. A full banking license was considered to be too restrictive for Securum to be able to fulfill its mandate and task. The mandate was both narrow—to work out the bad assets transferred to it only from Nordbanken—and broad; its management was given very broad powers to manage the process. The task was to determine whether and how the borrowers could be restructured both operationally and financially to reemerge as going concerns, and to execute such restructuring plans.

Despite 100 percent ownership by the state, the state did not assume the role of an active owner. It chose instead to entrust its operations to a board and a managing director composed largely of real estate professionals, with politicians and ministry officials in the minority.[8] Securum's independence was strengthened by its substantial equity injection, which was designed to preclude the entity from having to return to the state to ask for additional funding during its initially envisioned 15-year life span. It also established a number of subsidiary companies to handle specific types of assets, thus further insulating daily operations from political pressure.

Establishment and Early Years

The portfolio transferred to Securum consisted of over 3,000 loans to 1,274 companies (of which 790 were limited liability companies, the largest being Nobel Industries). The book value was SKr 67 billion, with a total transfer price of SKr 50 billion to account for loss reserves, and it represented about 20 percent of Nordbanken's total loan portfolio (table 4.5). Loans represented 90 percent of the portfolio, and the remainder was shares and real estate. The companies concerned were highly insolvent. Securum did not purchase its assets in

Table 4.5 Securum and Retriva's Portfolios

	Securum (Nordbanken)	Retriva (Gota)
Gross value of assets transferred (SKr)	67 billion	39 billion
Book value of assets transferred (SKr)	50 billion	16 billion
NPLs transferred as share of total loans (%)	21	45
Capitalization of AMC (SKr)	24 billion	3.8 billion

Note: AMC = asset management company; NPL = nonperforming loan.

exchange for any consideration. Instead, the loans together with the associated reserves were transferred to Securum and the government recapitalized Nordbanken directly.

The asset transfer process relied heavily on Nordbanken to select the assets to be transferred. Assets and collateral were valued throughout the autumn of 1992, with the support of external consultants and a large auditing firm. Owing to time restrictions, valuation of one-fifth of the assets was done using models that were based on the valuation of the other assets. The validity of documentation for loans and collateral was verified by Nordbanken and the process was overseen by an auditor appointed by Nordbanken's Board. The valuation methods used were validated by a committee comprising representatives of both Nordbanken and Securum.

Performance and Winding-up

Securum's strategy for disposal of assets was straightforward and effective. Companies with low profitability, unpaid interest, a low interest coverage ratio, a high debt/equity ratio, or no track record were filed for bankruptcy. Companies deemed to have potential were reorganized through mergers, acquisitions, and sales of assets. In addition, extensive measures were taken both to improve productivity and product development and to adjust prices and product quality.

This approach led to a large number of corporate insolvencies. Of the 790 companies with loans in Securum, some 70 percent were either liquidated or forced into bankruptcy. In part, this reflects the resolution method chosen. This may also reflect, to some extent, the varied quality of assets and companies transferred to Securum by Nordbanken. Securum was operating in a distressed-asset market involving several AMCs, often dealing with the same companies or conglomerates, most notably Nobel Industries. In the early stages of the crisis, the bank supervisor—often at the request of the banks—had brought all the banks to the same table to facilitate a coordinated effort for the resolution of a complex case. In later stages, the coordination of the resolution process was left entirely to the banks and their AMCs.

Securum became de facto the largest real estate company in Sweden. In May 1996, Gota Bank's AMC Retriva was merged into Securum. The combined entity owned over 2,000 commercial real estate properties valued at SKr 15–20 billion, representing 1–2 percent of the entire commercial real estate stock in Sweden.

Properties were sold on an individual basis, grouped together in larger packages, or as whole property companies. The preferred method of sale for individual properties and packages of properties was sale by private treaty through direct negotiations with selected potential buyers. Whole property companies were sold through initial public offerings (IPOs) on the Stockholm (four transactions) and London (one transaction) stock exchanges. Although these IPOs provided substantial returns to Securum, they accounted for less than half of the assets disposed. These transactions were attractive, as they disposed of a large number of properties through the sale of shares, thus avoiding further depression of real estate values.

In contrast to the RTC, Securum did not sell properties by auctions. Among the reasons put forth are concerns regarding the length of time it would have taken to sell such a great number of properties by this method; the difficulty of putting together suitable packages of properties to maximize their return; the potential for depressing prices by bringing such a large number of properties to market; and the relatively small size of the market in Sweden, which would make it difficult to find a sufficient number of qualified buyers, coupled with the general lack of financing for potential purchasers at that time (Englund, 1999).

Initially, the time horizon for Securum's workout process was estimated at 10 to 15 years; however, the state expressed a preference for a shorter life span. Securum's board proposed in September 1995 that the company be wound down by mid-1997. The liquidation process for the remaining assets was accelerated; the majority of real estate divestitures took place in 1996 (25 percent) and 1997 (60 percent). The parliament dissolved Securum in June 1997.

By the time of its closure, Securum had disposed of 98 percent of its assets. The remaining properties, worth SKr 2 billion, were transferred to two state-owned holding companies, Vasakronan and Venantius, which continued the disposition process. Upon closure, Securum returned approximately SKr 14 billion, or 48 percent of its capitalization, to the government.

Various calculations have been presented at different times on how much the banking crisis of the 1990s cost the Swedish state and economy. The out-of-pocket net cost for the Swedish state at the end of the crisis in 1997 has been estimated at SKr 35 billion. However, should one extend the time horizon further until 2000, a marginally positive result would be the outcome, largely due to the increase in the value of the government's ownership in Nordbanken (that is, Nordea) and the privatization proceeds from those shares (Lybeck, 1993).

Another indirect cost of the banking crisis and the actions of the Swedish state in support of Nordbanken and Gota and their AMCs Securum and Retriva was the impact on the banking market, interestingly even beyond Sweden's borders. Other banks in Sweden and in other Nordic countries, faced stiff competition from a well-capitalized and cleaned-up Nordbanken (later Nordea) while they were still recovering from the crisis, either through their own efforts or with the support of their respective governments. Although it is obvious that the ample injection of capital made it easier for Nordbanken to play a leading role in the

Public Asset Management Companies • http://dx.doi.org/10.1596/978-1-4648-0874-6

structural transformation of the banking market in the Nordic countries following their respective crises, it is difficult to estimate the true impact on competition in a longer-term perspective.

Lessons Learned

The Swedish bank restructuring model in general and Securum in particular are
considered to have been highly successful. They have served as a best practice
model, with variations adopted in many subsequent crises. Yet, the Securum
model is not easily replicable in other countries. At least three factors very
specific to Sweden explain the success of the model:

* The buildup to the crisis was quite rapid consequent to domestic policy
  choices, resulting in quite homogeneous problem portfolios in the large banks,
  comprising primarily commercial real estate assets.
* As an advanced industrialized economy Sweden had—for the most part—an
  enabling legal, regulatory, and institutional framework and transparency in
  place suitable for crisis resolution.
* Sweden's relatively rapid and smooth recovery from the banking crisis was
  greatly helped by the coinciding strong economic recovery in the global markets. Swedish markets, specifically, were also helped along by the new variable
  currency regime, through which the central bank introduced a stability-pro-
  viding inflation-targeting regime in 1992.

Nonetheless, Securum's experience provides useful generic lessons:

* Securum was an integral part of a well-designed bank restructuring program
  that simultaneously addressed weaknesses in both the banks and the borrowers. Built around the core principle of saving banks and companies, not
  their owners, it was easy for both the public and the politicians to understand.
* Securum's incorporation as an ordinary company was crucial to its success.
  Because it was not subject to bank regulation and supervision, it was free to
  operate as a normal commercial, profit-making enterprise and to own, operate, and take whatever actions necessary to maximize the value of its properties. It had no social objectives. Its mandate was strictly limited to recovering
  the Nordenbanken (and later Gota) assets. Securum was staffed by professionals, not bureaucrats, who had experience in restructuring, operating, and
  selling companies. Its work program was simple and direct: obtain ownership
  of the property; improve its value; and sell. The ability to place the properties
  in subsidiary companies not only further insulated Securum from the possi-
  bility of political interference but also enabled it to group similar properties
  together for better management and ease of packaging for sale.
* Asset recovery began early in the process. Once the bad bank concept was
  selected, Nordenbanken's bad assets were moved into a subsidiary, Securum,

and the resolution process began. By the time that Securum was spun off, the bulk of the companies had already been either placed in bankruptcy or liquidated. This undoubtedly preserved value as the problems were addressed at an early stage when recovery is most likely.

- Securum and its private sector counterparts benefited from a strong enabling framework. Sweden was an industrialized country with sufficient resources to fund the restructuring program. It prided itself on a history of strong corporate governance, personal integrity, and the rule of law. The government had a history of responsible ownership of state-owned enterprises, and government institutions were respected. The legal prerequisites for a successful AMC were in place, and no special legal powers were required. Loans could be transferred without the borrower's permission; Securum could obtain clear title to the collateral and assumed all the rights of the former lender with respect to enforcement and other actions; and there was an orderly and effective insolvency process in place. Thus it was able to proceed with its work in a timely manner without having to wait for special powers to be enacted or legal reforms put in place.

Notes

1. The rest of the failed institutions (1,617) were insured and resolved by the Federal Deposit Insurance Corporation (FDIC). As such, they are not the subject of this case study.

2. Between June 1979 and late 1980, short-term interest rates rose by 11 percentage points, from 9.1 to 20.5 percent.

3. The problem was further exacerbated by many borrowers' ability to transfer their existing low-rate mortgage to the new owner upon the sale of the property. The "due on sale" mortgage provisions were not uniformly enacted until 1982.

4. Under the program, an S&L received a promissory note from the FDIC representing a portion of its current period losses in exchange for certificates that were considered part of the institution's capital for reporting and regulatory purposes. Of the 29 savings banks in the program, 22 required no further assistance, 7 required additional assistance, of which 4 repaid all assistance, and 3 were merged into healthy institutions.

5. The RTC was required to give a right of first refusal to tenants before selling one- to four-family residences and to give limited preference to purchase offers from non-profit organizations, government agencies, and others that would provide housing for homeless individuals and families.

6. As the FDIC markets institutions prior to closure, the process is subject to a high degree of confidentiality.

7. Performing loans were outsourced to loan servicers.

8. The chairman of the board was a chief executive officer (CEO) of a state-owned company; other members included the CEO of Securum (formerly deputy CEO of Nordbanken), a representative of the Ministry of Finance, and three independent directors chosen from the private sector.

CHAPTER 5

The Second Generation: KAMCO, IBRA, Danaharta, and the SDIF

Korea Asset Management Corporation (KAMCO), Republic of Korea

Context of the Use of KAMCO

In the fall of 1997, Korea experienced a twin currency and banking crisis. As in Indonesia, strong macroeconomic performance masked structural weaknesses in both the financial and corporate sectors, which left the economy exposed to external shocks, most notably financial contagion and the sudden reversal of capital flows. These weaknesses included the build-up of maturity mismatches and foreign currency risk, a weak financial sector, ineffective supervision and regulation, and an overleveraged corporate sector.

The liberalization of the financial system in the early 1990s led to rapid growth in domestic credit financed by large short-term capital inflows. Restrictions on short-term overseas borrowing by banks had been removed in 1993. However, tight controls remained in place, restricting access to medium-to long-term financing and capital markets. As a result, large maturity mismatches built up within the system as Korean financial institutions relied heavily on lower-cost short-term overseas borrowings to finance long-term domestic investments. At the end of 1996, the banking sector's external debt amounted to US\$100 billion, 63 percent of Korea's total foreign debt. Short-term borrowings by banks accounted for 81 percent of the country's total short-term external debt. Korean banks, however, felt little need to hedge their exchange rate risk as the won: dollar rate was tightly managed within a very narrow range.

Korea's financial system lacked a strong commercial focus. Risk management and credit analysis skills had been hindered by the government's history of intervention in the financial sector (for example, directed lending and appointment of senior managers). Lending decisions relied heavily on collateral and intercompany guarantees rather than on a proper assessment of risk and projected cash flows. Banks continued to finance corporate expansion into less profitable areas and created excess capacity. Increasing competition from nonbank financial institutions coupled with the artificially low cost of foreign borrowings impeded the proper pricing of risk and bank earnings. High operating costs weighed on profitability. Returns on capital, assets, and the capital adequacy ratio had all declined in the three years preceding the crisis (table 5.1).

Weak and fragmented prudential regulation and supervision masked problems within the financial sector. Loan classification standards and provisioning (box 5.1) as well as accounting and disclosure standards (for both banks and corporates) did not meet international standards, making it difficult to accurately assess risk. Banks' risk concentrations were poorly monitored, leading to large exposures to conglomerates that were heavily leveraged and dependent on bank financing. In addition, the bulk of corporate bonds issued carried a bank guarantee that exposed the financial system to even more corporate risk. Regulatory forbearance was common, making enforcement nontransparent and undermining the credibility of the system. These problems were compounded by the division of supervisory responsibilities between the Bank of Korea (BOK; for commercial banks) and the Ministry of Finance (for specialized banks and nonbank financial institutions). This led to regulatory arbitrage in the form of less stringent regulatory requirements on nonbanks, which competed directly with the commercial banks and expanded their activities.

The perception that the government would not allow major banks or large Korean *chaebols* to fail led to substantial moral hazard. Prior to the crisis, the

Table 5.1 Selected Financial Sector Indicators

	1994	1995	1996
Net income (US$ billion)	1,048.2	867.8	846.9
Return on capital (%)	6.38	4.66	4.33
Return on assets (%)	0.46	0.30	0.27
CAR	10.6	9.3	9.1

Source: Balino and Ubide (1999).
Note: CAR = capital adequacy ratio.

Box 5.1 Korean Standards for Loan Classification and Provisioning

Nonperforming loans (NPLs) were defined as loans that had been in arrears for six months or longer (versus the international standard of three months or more).

Bad loans were defined as that portion of NPLs not covered by collateral.

The classification was based on the loan's servicing record and the availability of collateral rather than an assessment of the borrower's future repayment capacity.

Banks were required to set aside provisions for loan losses at the end of the fiscal year in an amount equal to 100 percent of expected losses. Provisioning levels were based on loan classifications: 0.5 percent for normal credits; 1 percent for precautionary credits; 20 percent for substandard loans; and 100 percent for doubtful or loss loans.

Losses, however, were "not expected" to be in excess of 2 percent of total loans. Loss reserves in excess of 2 percent were not tax deductible.

government had never allowed a bank or a large *chaebol* to fail. Insolvent banks were either taken over by the government, forced to restructure with public funds, or merged with a healthy bank. This led depositors to believe that their deposits were implicitly insured, although the partial deposit insurance scheme was insufficiently funded to provide adequate coverage. Government bailouts of distressed companies, shielding owners and managers from the consequences of their bad decisions, led to excessive risk taking and substantial overcapacity within the corporate sector.

Problems in the corporate sector mirrored those of the financial sector. Because government policy favored debt over equity financing, the *chaebols* (like their banks) relied on short-term borrowing from banks to finance their long-term investment projects. They were also extraordinarily highly leveraged, with debt-to-equity ratios exceeding 400 percent for most. The reliance on cross-guarantees and cross-equity investments within the *chaebol* led to nontransparent corporate decision made by owners, typically a family, with little of their own capital at risk. Korean corporate financial statements did not conform to internationally accepted accounting and auditing standards, and prevented effective market discipline.

Problems began to surface in early 1997. With the region-wide slowdown in export growth during the latter part of 1996, problems within the corporate sector began to surface in early 1997 with the collapse of several chaebols and rising small and medium-sized business failures. In July 1997, several Korean banks were placed on a negative credit outlook by credit rating agencies due to concerns about declining corporate earnings and the true (versus reported) levels of NPLs within the system (box 5.2). International banks began to selectively reduce their credit lines to banks, forcing the government to announce a blanket guarantee on foreign borrowings by Korean banks in August 1997. Regional sentiment continued to worsen over the next few months and on October 24th,

---

Box 5.2 Estimating the True Magnitude of NPLs

Prior to the crisis, reported nonperforming loans (NPLs) had averaged about 5 percent of total loans, as only loans in arrears of six months or more had been classified as NPLs. When the government applied internationally accepted standards to estimate the true magnitude of NPLs at the end of March 1998, the figure increased dramatically, to US$98 billion (27 percent of gross domestic product—GDP), or about 18 percent of total loans. The government decided to target US$83 billion of these NPLs with an estimated market value of approximately 50 percent for immediate disposal. These loans included US$56 billion of loans in arrears in excess of six months plus a portion of those loans classified as "precautionary" (in arrears three to six months). Approximately half of the loans were to be disposed of by the financial institutions themselves, either through calling the loan or selling the collateral; the remainder were to be purchased by Korea Asset Management Corporation (KAMCO). These estimates proved overly optimistic. In the end, KAMCO purchased NPLs with a face value of US$91 billion for US$33 billion, or 36 percent of face value.

Source: He (2004, 7)

Standard and Poor's downgraded Korea's credit rating from AA– to A+, resulting in capital flight and the wholesale withdrawal of credit lines. The BOK's intervention in the foreign exchange markets proved ineffective and on November 21, the government requested an International Monetary Fund program.

The swift resolution of NPLs was a critical component of the government's crisis resolution strategy. In November 1997, the government announced that a program of NPL acquisition would be an integral part of its financial sector restructuring program. Other elements of the program included liquidity support; a blanket deposit guarantee, closure of nonviable institutions, recapitalization of systemically important institutions, strengthening of prudential regulation and supervision to bring it in line with international standards, and the introduction of a program to enhance and accelerate badly needed corporate restructuring.

Mandate and Legal Powers

The government chose to house the NPL program (that is, AMC function) within an existing entity rather than create a new institution. KAMCO was established in 1962 as a subsidiary of the Korea Development Bank (KDB) for the purpose of liquidating KDB's nonperforming assets. In 1966, it began to purchase NPLs from other financial institutions, and over the years it developed into a specialized real estate management company. Beginning in the 1980s, its mission was further expanded to the management and disposition of state-owned properties. In November 1997, KAMCO was once again reorganized pursuant to the "Act on Efficient Management of Nonperforming Assets of Financial Institutions and Establishment of Korea Asset Management Corporation" (the KAMCO Act) as a public nonbank financial corporation, under the supervision of the newly established consolidated regulatory and supervisory agency, the Financial Supervisory Commission (FSC). The government directly owns 42.8 percent of KAMCO; the remaining 47.2 percent is split equally between KDB (a state-owned bank) and other financial institutions.[1]

KAMCO's mandate was narrowly focused on the acquisition, management, and disposition of NPLs. Under its enabling legislation, in addition to its traditional duties, KAMCO was empowered to support financial institutions through the purchase of NPLs; perform the role of a "bad bank" that engages in corporate restructuring by extending loans, debt-equity swaps, and payment guarantees; and recover public funds through the efficient management and disposal of its assets. Unlike many AMCs, it was not directly engaged in the restructuring or recapitalization of banks.

The KAMCO Act required NPL resolution activities to be conducted through the Non-Performing Asset Management Fund (the NPA Fund) and did not specify a sunset date. KAMCO, in effect, acted as the manager of the NPA Fund, which had a separate legal identity and different funding sources than KAMCO. Although the act set no specific sunset date for resolution activities, it did limit the NPA Fund's ability to issue bonds and purchase NPLs to five years (that is, until November 2002).

KAMCO is governed by an 11-member Management Supervisory Committee. Membership consists of the managing director of KAMCO; representatives from the Ministry of Finance and Economy (MOFE), the Ministry of Planning and Budgeting, the FSC, and the Korea Deposit Insurance Corporation; the deputy governor of the KDB; two representatives from the banking industry nominated by the chairman of the Korea Federation of Banks; and three professionals recommended by the managing director, including an attorney-at-law, a certified public accountant (CPA) or a certified tax accountant, and a university professor or a doctorate holder who works for a research institute. In addition, KAMCO's performance with respect to the NPA Fund was monitored by the Public Fund Oversight Committee, led by the MOFE.

KAMCO was not granted any special powers. The Korean legal system was relatively mature and already provided for the clean transfer of titles and priority in asset transactions. However, KAMCO was granted a few special privileges in order to facilitate the resolution of NPLs, including exemption from financial transaction taxes. In addition, Korea took a number of steps to strengthen its legal and regulatory framework surrounding corporate restructuring. For example, it amended three bankruptcy-related laws in 1998 (the Firm Liquidation Law, the Court Mediation Law, and the Bankruptcy Law) to enhance creditors' rights, provide an out-of-court restructuring process, and improve the efficiency and speed of the liquidation or bankruptcy of troubled companies.

Funding

The NPA Fund's principal source of financing for NPL purchases was the issuance of government-guaranteed bonds. KAMCO raised a total of US$18 billion (won 21.5 trillion) through the issuance of US$17.1 billion (won 20.5 trillion) of bonds, US$478 million (won 500 billion) from assessments on financial institutions in proportion to their holdings of NPLs, and a US$417 million (won 500 billion) loan from KDB. KAMCO also recycled US$15 billion of recovered funds to support its purchases. The KAMCO bonds typically had a one- to five-year maturity, carried a mixture of fixed and floating coupons, and yielded a market rate of interest.[2] As the bonds were fully guaranteed by the Korean government, they carried a 0 percent risk weight for regulatory capital purposes. This provided a strong incentive for banks to sell NPLs to quickly improve their capital base and meet the minimum 8 percent capital adequacy ratio.

Asset Acquisition and Disposition

KAMCO was authorized to purchase nonperforming loans from a wide variety of financial institutions. Although the bulk of NPLs were purchased from commercial banks (56 percent by face value), KAMCO also purchased assets from merchant banks, investment trusts, and insurance companies, as well as securities firms (table 5.2). Loans eligible for purchase were broadly defined as those classified substandard and below whose security rights and transfer were legally executable. Priority was given to the purchase of NPLs whose removal was considered critical to the restructuring of the originating institution as well as NPLs that had multiple creditors.

Table 5.2 NPL Acquisition by Seller

Seller	Face Value (US$ billion)	Purchase Price (US$ billion)	Purchase Price as Share of Face Value (%)
Banks	51.52	20.60	40
Merchant banks	2.92	1.35	46
Guarantee insurance	5.88	1.46	25
Life insurance	0.25	0.06	23
Securities	0.12	0.07	57
Mutual savings	0.44	0.18	40
Foreign financial institutions	4.18	1.75	42
Financial resolution entities under KDIC	5.65	0.70	12
Investment trust companies	18.58	6.99	38
Others	2.22	0.01	0
Total	91.75	33.16	36

Source: He (2004, 13).
Note: KDIC = Korea Deposit Insurance Corporation; NPL = nonperforming loans.

KAMCO purchased over 300,000 NPLs with a face value of won 110 trillion (approximately US$92 billion), representing 9 percent of financial sector assets or some 20 percent of gross domestic product (GDP). Given the disproportionate share of lending extended to a few large *chaebols*, it is not surprising that roughly 1 percent of borrowers accounted for 90 percent of the face value of these loans. The purchases were classified as follows:

• Ordinary loans: loans to companies that continued to operate
• Special loans: restructured loans under court-supervised receivership
• Daewoo loans: acquired mostly in 2000 in the wake of the collapse of the Daewoo Group
• Workout loans: loans to companies in the out-of-court workout programs

Some 85 percent of the assets were purchased by the end of 2000, with secured special loans and Daewoo loans, the two largest categories of purchases, each representing 32 percent of the total. Secured ordinary loans accounted for an additional 18 percent of total purchases (table 5.3).

On average, KAMCO purchased NPLs for 36 percent of their face value. The actual discount varied greatly depending on the type of loan, with the highest prices paid for secured ordinary loans (67 percent) and the lowest prices for unsecured ordinary loans (11 percent) (table 5.3). The variation in prices paid for loans bought from different lenders did not appear to be significant, except that loans bought from institutions to be closed and resolved by the Korea Deposit Insurance Corporation (KDIC) were priced much lower than loans bought from institutions that were going concerns. KAMCO paid more on average for NPLs purchased before mid-1999. After that, as the government adopted a more uniform market-oriented pricing mechanism based on the present value of projected cash flows, prices became more realistic, facilitating the development of the private market for distressed corporate debt.

Table 5.3 KAMCO NPL Purchases by Asset Type

Asset Type	Face Value (US$, billion)	Amount Paid (US$, billion)	Price as Share of Face Value (%)	Percent of Total Paid
Ordinary loan secured	9	6	67	18
Ordinary loan (unsecured)	17	2	11	6
Special loan (secured)	22	11	47	32
Special loan (unsecured)	12	3	29	11
Daewoo loan	30	10	36	32
Workout loan	2	1	23	1
Total	**92**	**33**	**36**	**100**

Source: He (2004, 12).
Note: KAMCO = Korea Asset Management Corporation; NPL = nonperforming loans.

Table 5.4 Pricing of NPL Purchases

Type of Loan	Date	Pricing Formula Secured	Pricing Formula Nonsecured	Price Determination
Ordinary Loans	November 97–July 98	70–75 percent of valid collateral value [a]	Doubtful: 10–20 percent of face value Assumed loss: 1–3 percent of face value	subject to ex post adjustment
	Since September 98	45 percent of collateral value [b]	3 percent of face value	fixed at the beginning
Special Loans	November 97–July 98	70–75 percent of face value	20–60 percent of face value	subject to ex post adjustment
	September 98–June 99	45 percent of collateral value [b]		
	Since July 99	Present value of projected cash flows [c]		fixed at the beginning

Source: He (2004, 15), from KAMCO.
Note: KAMCO = Korea Asset Management Corporation; NPL = nonperforming loans.
a. Valid collateral value is the least of "appraisal value–senior lines," "face value," or "maximum collateral amount."
b. Collateral value = appraisal value–senior lines.
c. Discount rate = basic discount rate + credit risk spread + maturity risk spread.

KAMCO's pricing evolved over time. KAMCO began purchasing assets in late November 1997 (table 5.4). As the markets were in turmoil and it was important to move quickly to stabilize the financial sector, KAMCO used bulk purchases to speed up the transfer process. Under this methodology, which remained in place until September 1998, the final settlement price was roughly equivalent to the loan loss provisioning rates then in effect and was subject to the negotiation of ex post individual settlement agreements. A central feature of these agreements was a recourse arrangement or put/call option that allowed either KAMCO to return (put) or the seller to request (call) the return of the loan(s) if the initial bulk purchase price and the eventual resolution or evaluation price turned out to differ substantially. As the markets became more stable, both KAMCO and the selling institutions gained more time, experience, and better market information to more accurately price transactions. After September 1998, KAMCO abandoned the put/call or recourse feature in favor of purchasing NPLs for a fixed price, which was calculated using a formula that reflected the specific characteristics and terms and conditions of the loan. Sellers were free to decide if they wished to accept the price.

KAMCO was directed by the government to purchase Daewoo bonds held by foreign creditors and the investment trust companies at inflated prices. Although their purchase price was on average only 32.6 percent of face value (for assets other than secured commercial paper), the expected recovery rate on these claims was much lower. However, the government made a policy decision to pay a premium to these creditors in order to facilitate a speedier out-of-court restructuring process for these loans (box 5.3).

Box 5.3 Facilitating Corporate Restructuring

Many countries affected by the crisis, including Korea, adopted formal frameworks to expedite the out-of-court restructuring of distressed debt. Although the design of each country's framework depended on its specific circumstances, all were based on the consensual workout approach known as the London Approach, pioneered by the Bank of England.

In the case of Korea, under the guidance of the Financial Supervisory Commission (FSC), 210 local financial institutions agreed to pursue a contractual approach to out-of-court workouts as an alternative to unsupervised "bankruptcy avoidance" loans (that is, bailouts) and court-supervised insolvency. These institutions signed a corporate restructuring agreement (CRA) that provided for a one- to three-month standstill (depending on due diligence requirements), that could be extended for one month; a creditors' committee led by a lead creditor, typically the chaebol's lead bank; a 75 percent threshold for creditors' approval of a workout agreement; a seven-person Corporate Restructuring Coordination Committee, selected by signatories, to provide workout guidelines and arbitrate differences in cases where creditors could not approve a workout plan after three votes. The CRA also incorporated penalties of up to 30 percent of the amount of the credit or up to 50 percent of the cost of noncompliance if a signatory failed to comply with an approved workout agreement or committee arbitration decision.

In addition, Korea adopted a series of policy measures to support corporate restructuring, including the following:

- Tax exemptions and reductions to encourage merger and acquisition (M&A) transactions
- A series of incentives to encourage foreign direct investment
- Modification of labor standards to allow layoffs in corporate restructuring and M&As
- An increase in the limits on the amount of converted corporate equity that financial institutions could hold
- Progressive limitations on interest deductibility for corporate taxes
- The gradual adoption of international accounting standards
- Improved disclosure and reporting requirements for public companies
- The creation of dedicated bankruptcy courts
- Enhanced corporate governance requirements for public companies

Source: Lieberman et al. (2005, 67).

Asset Disposition

KAMCO's overall resolution strategy combined rapid disposition and medium-term debt workout and restructuring. KAMCO focused on the timely disposition of assets with limited recovery potential while restricting workout and restructuring to those assets whose recovery value could be increased. This strategy was deemed appropriate given the dominance of the *chaebols* in the Korean economy. In addition to traditional methods such as competitive auctions, collection of rescheduled repayments, and recourse to the original seller, KAMCO also developed innovative techniques that included asset-based securitization (ABS), international bidding, and joint venture partnerships (table 5.5). KAMCO's disposition strategies can be divided into four broad categories with the choice of method depending on the nature and size of the NPL:

- Bulk (pool) sale of NPLs through creation of a domestic and international ABS market and competitive international auctions: Bulk sales were attractive as they resolved a large number of loans, resulted in substantial cash flows, and attracted foreign investment through a competitive international bidding process. KAMCO pioneered the use of ABS which, in their most basic form, involved the transfer of NPLs to an special-purpose vehicle (SPV) which then issued securities, payable from the collection of the NPLs, in the public market. KAMCO issued its first domestic ABS in 1999, followed in 2000 by an international issue[3] in the Eurobond market. In all, KAMCO issued 14 ABS transactions, accounting for 18 percent of the face value of loan resolutions (excluding recoveries from recourse and cancellation transactions) while recovering 12 percent of the face value of the underlying securities and 99 percent of their purchase price.
- Establishment of joint ventures: KAMCO sold large portfolios to joint ventures and equity partnerships. These sales, conducted through a competitive

Table 5.5 KAMCO NPL Resolution by Method, End of December 2002

Resolution Method	Face Value (US$ billion)	Purchase Price (US$ billion)	Recovery (US$ billion)	Share of Face Value (%)
International bidding	5.07	1.09	1.34	26.4
ABS issuance	6.68	3.52	3.48	52.1
Sale to AMC	2.15	0.55	0.77	35.8
Sale to CRC	1.54	0.3	0.56	36.4
Individual loan sales	2.16	0.53	0.76	35.2
Court auction, public sales	6.92	2.19	2.69	38.9
Collection	10.54	3.56	4.94	46.9
Daewoo	2.73	1.86	2.22	81.3
Subtotal	**37.8**	**13.6**	**16.75**	**44.3**
Recourse and cancellation	16.06	8.47	8.47	52.7
Total	**53.86**	**22.07**	**25.22**	**46.8**

Source: KAMCO (2003): slide 16.
Note: ABS = asset-based securitization; KAMCO = Korea Asset Management Corporation; NPL = nonperforming loans; CRC = corporate restructuring company.

international auction process, brought in much-needed international expertise in corporate restructuring and technology. The joint venture partnerships, in which KAMCO typically held a 50 percent ownership interest, were established to manage and dispose of real estate (AMC joint ventures) or to enhance recovery values through corporate restructuring joint ventures. This technique not only served as a knowledge transfer vehicle for KAMCO but also provided it with the opportunity to participate in the upside if recoveries exceeded certain levels. It also helped to reduce local domestic political resistance to sales to foreigners.

- Foreclosure, public auctions, and individual loan sales: KAMCO also sold assets through the courts (foreclosure), by public auctions, and directly. The latter method was generally reserved for large assets such as corporates.
- Loan Workout or Restructuring: Restructuring was conducted either through the informal out-of-court restructuring framework (the preferred method) or under the less efficient court ordered program.

As of the end of December 2002,[4] KAMCO had resolved US$54 billion (approximately 60 percent) of its US$92 billion in assets, at an average recovery rate of 46.8 percent of face value. It should be noted, however, that this includes US$8.47 billion of recoveries at 100 percent of face value on loans subject to recourse. If these amounts are excluded, recoveries are reduced to US$37.8 billion or 41 percent of acquired assets, for an average recovery rate of 44 percent. Roughly 50 percent of the loans by face value were resolved through traditional workout practices, court actions, and public sales, and another 40 percent through the use of the more innovative methods. All methods—with the exception of asset securitization, which broke even—resulted in KAMCO recovering more than the purchase price of the assets.

Performance
KAMCO's overall performance is best described as mixed, with large operating expenses erasing strong recovery efforts. By the end of 2002, KAMCO had generated some US$3.2 billion in profit from asset sales. However, these funds failed to reach KAMCO's bottom line owing to high operating expenses, which averaged close to 30 percent of collections (versus less than 15 percent of collections for the RTC. The fund showed a negative equity of approximately US$5.7 billion. In recognition that KAMCO would be unable to fully repay its bonds, the government converted KAMCO's short-term maturities into treasury bonds with the remainder of the longer-term debt to be serviced by increases in the deposit insurance premium and future recoveries. In return for this assistance, KAMCO assumed responsibility for payment of interest on the obligations.

On a more positive note, KAMCO's new techniques to maximize recovery values created the distressed-debt market, providing new avenues for banks and other financial institutions to better manage their credit risk. KAMCO's use of securitization, sales to joint ventures and corporate restructuring vehicles, and a competitive international bidding process brought in funding and corporate restructuring expertise. On the basis of these results, banks began to sell their NPLs directly to foreign investors, increasing competition which, in turn, resulted in increasing asset values. The introduction of ABS led to further development of the capital markets.

Lessons Learned

The KAMCO experience clearly demonstrates the importance of strong domestic political consensus and public support. When the crisis hit, there was broad political and public consensus regarding the need to use and quickly recover public funds to stabilize the financial system. The idea of an AMC was first raised in April 1997, and by the end of November, KAMCO had acquired its first assets, within days of the passage of its enabling legislation. The public's consensus on the need to reduce the government debt also helped focus KAMCO's efforts on the rapid disposition of its assets as well as profit maximization.

An AMC plays an important role in the creation of a market for distressed assets. When KAMCO began operations, there was no market for distressed assets in Korea. As KAMCO designed products to meet the needs of investors and aggressively sought out foreign investors, the distressed-asset market began to function, bringing fresh liquidity into the market along with technical expertise. As information flows improved and the adoption of international accounting standards allowed for better risk assessments, competition increased and pricing began to improve as well. By the end of the crisis, an active market had developed for distressed debt, providing financial institutions with another tool to manage risk.

Effective asset resolution requires a concurrent program of reforms to strengthen both the financial and the corporate sectors. Reform efforts traditionally have focused on improving prudential regulation and supervision, restructuring banks, and strengthening creditor rights. Korea's experience clearly shows that the corporate restructuring process is accelerated by a concurrent program to improve corporate sector transparency and governance, facilitate mergers and acquisitions, create a distressed-asset market, and strengthen the development of the domestic capital market for both equity and bonds.

Indonesian Bank Restructuring Authority (IBRA), Indonesia

Context of the Creation of IBRA

In the years preceding the 1997 Asian financial crisis, Indonesia fully participated in the "Asian Miracle." Incomes rose substantially; inflation and food prices remained stable; the economy became more diversified and export oriented; and significant capital inflows fueled a surge in imports and investment, particularly in the real estate sector. Given its more stable macroeconomic policies (a liberal capital account regime, financial deregulation, and a stable macroeconomic framework), Indonesia was believed to be well positioned to weather the regional currency crisis which began in Thailand in mid-1997.

But multiple fault lines lay hidden underneath the encouraging macroeconomic data. Exports had begun to fall rapidly toward the end of 1996. Financial deregulation had led to a rapid expansion in the number of banks[5] but regulation was outdated, supervision lax, and enforcement largely nonexistent. Many of the banks were owned by the conglomerates, which viewed them as little more than their funding sources. Corruption was pervasive throughout all levels of public, corporate, and private society. This led to the routine misallocation of both public and private funds (bank loans) for personal use.

After unsuccessful attempts to stabilize the rupiah, Indonesia was forced to request an International Monetary Fund (IMF) program in early October 1997. As part of its initial assessment, the IMF conducted a review of 92 banks, representing 85 percent of the sector's total assets.[6] The results revealed that 34 banks (5 percent of total assets) were insolvent by international standards and an additional 16 private banks (19 percent of total assets) exhibited various degrees of problems. Provisions to address these banks were included in the first IMF program. They focused on specific open bank resolution programs for eight state and regional development banks; the liquidation of 16 insolvent banks (with a 2.5 percent market share), notwithstanding that several were politically well connected[7] and placement of the remaining 16 weak but still solvent banks under conservatorship or intensive supervision.[8]

Initial public opinion was favorable to the closure of 16 insolvent banks in November 1997, but within several weeks confidence began to erode. Throughout December and early January, the banks began to experience deposit runs. Although several factors contributed, confidence in the program collapsed when it become known that President's Soeharto's son, whose Bank Andromeda was one of the 16 closed banks, had been effectively allowed to reopen his bank. The public saw this as business as usual, and the program's credibility was undermined.

What began as a currency crisis now turned into a full-blown banking crisis. Within the first year of the crisis, real GDP contracted by 13 percent; the rupiah depreciated by 80 percent, and inflation had accelerated to about 70 percent per annum (IMF 2004, 3). This forced the authorities to take extraordinary measures to provide liquidity and capital and restructure the banks under the auspices of the newly created IBRA. Overall, it is estimated that the crisis cost about 51 percent of GDP (table 5.6), making this one of the world's costliest bank restructuring programs.

Public Asset Management Companies • http://dx.doi.org/10.1596/978-1-4648-0874-6

Table 5.6 Cost of the Banking Crisis

	Rupiah (trillion)	Share of 2000 GDP (%)	US$ (billion)
Total cost	650	51	77
Recap bonds	430	34	51
Liquidity support	220	17	26
Assets assumed	533	42	63
Of which NPLs	347	27	41
Recoveries	151	12	18

Source: IMF (2004).
Note: GDP = gross domestic product; IMF = International Monetary Fund; NPL = nonperforming loans.

Box 5.4 IBRA's Extrajudicial Powers

- Right to transfer loans to and from Indonesian Bank Restructuring Authority (IBRA) without consent of borrower
- Right to investigate and examine borrowers as well as members of the board of directors or board of commissioners, shareholders, and bank employees to acquire information that will further recovery efforts
- Right to freeze the assets of banks and their debtors, both within and outside of Indonesia
- Right to seize a debtor's assets through a special administrative rather than court procedure
- Right to review, change, terminate, or cancel contracts between banks and third parties that are deemed to have inflicted losses on IBRA

Mandate and Legal Powers

IBRA was created by presidential decree on January 26, 1998, for a period of five years[9] as a bank restructuring agency to administer the deposit guaranty and to intervene in and restructure banks declared unsound by the central bank (Bank Indonesia). The new agency was established direcly under the minister of finance and was headed by a chairman appointed by the president. Other key personnel were appointed by the minister of finance after consultation with the governor of the central bank. In addition, it was stipulated that upon its dissolution, remaining IBRA assets belonged to the state. IBRA was granted special powers to exercise its mandate.

The establishment of IBRA took over a year, during which period its mandate was further expanded to that of an AMC. It would be another eight months (October 1998) before Banking Law Amendments[10] were passed granting IBRA the legal powers necessary to exercise its responsibilities with respect to bank closure and restructuring and another four months (February 1999) before the necessary implementing regulations were enacted to allow it to use its special powers (box 5.4). During this time, IBRA's role was expanded to include (i) managing the NPLs from those banks that had been closed, nationalized, or jointly recapitalized by the government and their shareholders; and (ii) negotiating and managing settlement agreements with the controlling shareholders of the closed banks. IBRA did not purchase NPLs; instead, they were transferred in return for recapitalization or when IBRA closed a bank.

IBRA's initial mandate lacked clarity with respect to its role relative to Bank Indonesia. Within weeks of its establishment, Bank Indonesia moved to transfer to IBRA the supervision of 54 banks, amounting to some 37 percent of the sector.[11] However, IBRA's efforts to place staff on the banks' premises and enter into corrective memoranda of understanding with the banks were met with resistance as it lacked full legal authority for these actions. In addition, the lack of clear guidelines governing the division of supervisory responsibilities between Bank Indonesia and IBRA led to confusion within the public, the banks, and the organizations themselves as to the roles of the respective institutions. Ultimately, Bank Indonesia reassumed responsibility for supervision of the IBRA banks, and it was made clear that IBRA's role was limited to acting as Bank Indonesia's agent for the closure of banks and for the restructuring of weak banks.

Governance and transparency issues plagued IBRA throughout its life. The Banking Law Amendments and Implementing Regulations were largely silent regarding governance and transparency. Incremental changes were introduced, driven in large part by the World Bank and the IMF. The first was the creation of an Independent Review Committee to review the operations. Given its infrequent meetings and the limitation of its role to the after-the-fact review of decisions taken, it was largely ineffective. In 2000, a more formal board was established, the oversight committee, as well as an audit committee and ombudsman function. However, many transparency issues surfaced regarding the valuation of assets and recovery efforts.[12] Over time, IBRA showed improvements. Operating results were reported to the legislature; financial results were audited in accordance with generally accepted accounting principles and published; the budget was revised and approved on a gross basis; and IBRA's goals with respect to recoveries were publicly disclosed and tracked.

Funding
IBRA was funded directly from the Indonesian budget. Unlike many other AMCs, IBRA did not issue bonds. Instead, the bonds to recapitalize the banking sector were issued directly by the government. Annual recovery targets for IBRA were established and the proceeds, net of operating expenses, were remitted directly to the government to reduce the budget deficit.

Operational Issues
IBRA's organizational structure suffered from a silo mentality. Internally, IBRA organized itself around its three main business lines—bank restructuring, asset management (loan recovery), and shareholder settlements. Each department focused on its area of responsibility to the exclusion of the other operating divisions. This led to the development of a silo mentality, with each area maintaining its own internal databases and operating systems, resulting in data inconsistencies

and integrity problems that compromised financial data for both reporting and management purposes. Comprehensive policies and procedures governing the work of all areas were also incomplete. Over time, IBRA showed progress as corrective actions plans were developed and implemented but much valuable time and management attention was diverted during the process.

IBRA initially recorded its loan assets at book rather than market value. IBRA received its assets either from the closed banks or as part of the recapitalization program. Although the banks were required to write the loans down to the values indicated by the due diligence program before recapitalization, IBRA chose to record the loans at their gross, rather than net, book value, thereby seriously overestimating their realizable value. Public confidence was undermined as early sales showed losses rather than recoveries. Beginning with the 2000 year-end financial statements, IBRA's assets were more accurately described and shown in the notes.

Asset Disposition and Bank Sales

Throughout its lifetime, IBRA closed 54 banks, nationalized 24 banks, and held a majority stake in 6 jointly recapitalized banks. Mergers and sales were the primary resolution tools (table 5.7), although three of the nationalized banks were closed early in the restructuring process. Sales were originally projected to begin in 1999 and continue throughout IBRA's lifetime. However, the program was severely delayed by a combination of factors including delays in recapitalizing the banks, and in developing and implementing appropriate business plans, and unanticipated difficulties in merging the banks. IBRA also had to overcome significant resistance to the sale of the banks, particularly to foreign investors.

IBRA's first sale, BCA, (Bank Central Asia) finally took place in March 2002, with sales of the remaining banks following on a fairly regular basis thereafter.

Table 5.7 IBRA Bank Sales

Bank	Date	Share Sold (%)	Method	Proceeds (Rp trillion)	Price/Booka (Rp trillion)
BCA	March 2002	51	Strategic sale	5.6	1.1
Niaga	November 2002	51	Strategic sale	1.1	1.5
	Multipleb	20	Market placement	0.5	1.6
Danamon	May 2003	51	Strategic sale	3.0	1.3
	July 2003	20	Market placement	1.1	1.4
BII	December 2003	51	Strategic sale	2.1	1.3
	December 2003	20	Market placement	0.8	1.5
Lippo	February 2004	52	Strategic sale	1.2	1.0

Source: IMF (2004, 34).
Note: Excludes February 2004 sale of minority stakes (1–8 percent) in the banks, which raised Rp 1.5 trillion. IBRA = Indonesian Bank Restructuring Authority; IMF = International Monetary Fund; BII = Bank Internasional Indonesia.
a. Book value as of December before sale, except Niaga (December 2002) and Lippo (September 2003).
b. July–October 2002 and July–September 2003.

Banks were returned to private ownership (primarily foreign investor groups) through a transparent auction process, with minority stakes sold directly into the market or as blocks to the majority owner. In total, IBRA recovered some Rp 19 trillion from sale proceeds and dividends[13] from its equity holdings as compared with the Rp 9 trillion expended to recapitalize these banks and an additional Rp 9 trillion injected in BII (Bank Internasional Indonesia) and Permata to address liquidity shortfalls. In addition to the sales of their equity positions, IBRA also recovered an additional Rp 5.1 trillion from the sales at public auction of over 5,500 properties and other assets of the closed banks.

The Asset Management Unit managed NPLs with a book value of Rp 346.7 trillion (27 percent of 2000 GDP).[14] It was by far the largest of the IBRA units, employing 334 full-time and 3,400 temporary staff from the closed banks, supported by 221 legal and operational professionals (Lehman Brothers 2000, 26). IBRA's NPL portfolio, accounting for some 90 percent of NPLs in the system, was segmented by loan type with different resolution strategies applied to each category (table 5.8). The number of loans to manage, as well as the concentration of the portfolio, complicated IBRA's task.[15]

IBRA's goal of restructuring loans prior to sale was inconsistent with operational realities, forcing a shift to rapid asset disposition. IBRA was specifically charged with preserving and enhancing the value of the NPLs through loan restructuring, with a goal of either returning restructured performing loans to the banking sector or disposing of them through loan sales. This was motivated by the belief that its special enforcement powers would provide a greater incentive for borrowers to restructure; a desire to return performing, restructured loans to a banking sector that was badly in need of earning assets; and, a reluctance to sell assets, many of which included equity positions in Indonesia's corporates, to foreign investors. In addition, it was originally envisioned that IBRA would actively participate in the Jakarta Initiative Task Force (JITF; box 5.5). This focus

Table 5.8 IBRA Loan Portfolio by Type and Initial Resolution Strategy

Type	Accounts	Debtors	Debtors, Share of Total (%)	Total Book Value (Rp trillion)	Book Value (%)	Recovery Strategy
Retail/SME, < Rp 5 billion	313,760	294,414	98	29.4	8	Cash settlement with discounts, direct sales
Commercial, Rp 5–50 billion	7,239	1,996	1	27.0	8	Outsourced to BTO banks for restructuring, then sale
Corporate, > Rp 50 billion	52,626	1,867	1	290.3	84	Restructuring by IBRA, then sale
Total	**373,625**	**298,277**	**100**	**346.7**	**100**	

Source: IMF (2004, 29).
Note: IBRA = Indonesian Bank Restructuring Authority; IMF = International Monetary Fund.

Box 5.5 Jakarta Initiative Task Force

The Jakarta Initiative Task Force (JITF) framework was designed to facilitate a consensual out-of-court negotiating process for resolving corporate debt. Based on the London Approach, the JITF framework embodied generally accepted restructuring principles including the formation of creditors' committees, sharing of relevant information, voluntary "standstill" periods during which creditors refrain from pursuing their legal rights, and interim priority financing.

In an attempt to speed up the restructuring process, two additional enhancements were added. First, the JITF provided restructuring and mediation professionals to help the parties find mutually agreeable solutions. Second, the JITF was designed to be a one-stop shop to facilitate the regulatory applications required for restructuring plans. In this role, it could also recommend incentives for restructuring and removing obstacles related to matters such as taxation, legal lending limits, disclosure of financial information, and divestiture by banks of equity acquired in restructuring transactions.

In practice, restructuring under the JITF was slow, as it experienced the same obstacles as Indonesian Bank Restructuring Authority (IBRA) did. The consensual approach of the JITF negotiating framework did not work well in an environment where the legal system failed to pose a credible threat to recalcitrant debtors. It proved difficult to turn the one-stop forum into a reality, and coordination with IBRA was initially poor.

---

on restructuring, however, was inconsistent with the operational realities faced by IBRA. The sheer scope and volume of assets under management could not have been restructured and sold within the agency's limited five-year life span. And neither management nor staff had the requisite restructuring skills and experience.

In 2002, IBRA admitted that it was unlikely to accomplish its mandate and shifted its strategy to rapid asset disposition. Loan sales were conducted through a transparent, market-based process with the floor price determined by an in-house assessment of each loan's market value. Over its life, IBRA sold 60 percent of its NPL portfolio with 87 percent of the sales occurring between 2002 and 2004. The average net recovery rate was 22 percent, reflecting both the poor quality of the loans and the length of time before their sale.

The shareholder settlements unit actively pursued former bank owners who had misused liquidity support. A total of 44 bank owners were deemed to have been in violation of Bank Indonesia regulations with respect to their use of liquidity support. Like the Savings Deposit Insurance Fund (SDIF) in Turkey, IBRA sought to recover these funds by requiring the former owners to transfer assets with sufficient value to repay their obligations. Unlike the SDIF, however, IBRA did not have the benefit of special collection powers with respect to these sums. Nor did it receive full ownership rights, including the power of sale, due to documentation flaws and fears that full ownership might exceed its mandate. Its only tool or option was to place a representative on the board of the corporation, leaving the existing owners and managers in place with full access to and control over the assets. By the time of IBRA's closure, it had recovered only 22.4 percent of the Rp 130.3 trillion owed by former owners. A total of 28 of the former owners had met their obligations, 6 were in full compliance, and 10 were in legal proceedings.

Performance and Winding-up

IBRA closed at the end of February 2004, with a mixed track record. While it performed well as a bank resolution agency, its performance with respect to maximizing recoveries through loan restructuring and shareholder settlements was less successful. Nonetheless, during its six year life span IBRA recovered Rp 151 trillion or approximately 23 percent of the Rp 650 trillion cost of the crisis (table 5.9). At the date of closure, approximately Rp 275 trillion of remaining assets were transferred to a newly established AMC under the auspices of the Ministry of Finance. Some 60 percent of these assets were in litigation, while the remaining consisted of unsold NPLs and equity stakes in banks.

Lessons Learned

IBRA's experience offers valuable lessons about the problems that may be encountered in emerging markets when trying to adopt a resolution model that worked well in a developed country (Securum). Lessons learned included the following:

Indonesia lacked necessary prerequisites for an effective AMC. Effective AMCs require a strong enabling framework to support their efforts. A strong credit culture that fosters proper underwriting and documentation of loans, information sharing through credit bureaus regarding borrowers' credit histories, effective bank regulation and supervision to ensure banks are well capitalized, a legal framework for creditor rights and insolvency coupled with a strong legal and judicial framework, well-developed capital markets, and fiscal and

Table 5.9 IBRA Recoveries, 1998–2004 (Rp trillion)

Cash recoveries (gross)	**132.9**
NPLs (including debt service)	75.9
Shareholder settlement agreements[a]	26.8
Bank equity	19.0
Other	11.2
Bond recoveries	**18.2**
Total gross recoveries	**151.1**
Less operating expenses	(7.2)
Total net recoveries	**143.9**
Gross recoveries as percentage of cost of crisis	*23.2*

Source: IMF (2004, 35).
Note: IBRA = Indonesian Bank Restructuring Authority; IMF = International Monetary Fund;
NPL = nonperforming loans.
a. Excludes amount reclassified as "Other."

macroeconomic stability are all prerequisites for effective AMC and bank reso-lution. Indonesia possessed none of these.

Lack of consensus and political support undermined IBRA's efforts. The crisis coincided with a period of unprecedented political turmoil[16] which precluded the development of a strong consensus regarding IBRA's mandate and operation. Differences with respect to how best to maximize recoveries, a continuing reluc-tance to recognize the losses through the sale of assets (both at market values and to foreigners), and lack of support for strong enforcement of the shareholder settlement agreements undermined IBRA's efforts and resulted in lower recover-ies than might otherwise have been expected.

IBRA's special powers proved to be ineffective in the face of the continued weak legal and judicial framework. In an attempt to overcome the lack of an effective creditor rights regime and a dysfunctional court system, IBRA was granted special powers designed to expedite the recovery process. However, they proved to be ineffective as the few attempts IBRA made to exercise these powers were overruled by the judiciary. Thus, the largest borrowers and shareholders had little incentive to enter into meaningful settlement negotiations. The value of the loans was also negatively affected by the uncertainties surrounding a creditor's ability to collect its debt in a timely manner.

Governance and transparency are crucial to ensuring credibility. As the spirit of "reformasi" spread in the early months after the fall of Soeharto in May 1998, IBRA represented a new approach to doing business in Indonesia. Unburdened by the old corruption practices, it was to serve as a leader in strengthening busi-ness practices. But a general lack of accountability and transparency with respect to its operations coupled with political interference in many loan restructurings soon led to a perception of business as usual and harmed IBRA's credibility. Over time, weaknesses were corrected but IBRA never regained full credibility and its actions continued to be questioned.

IBRA's mandate was overly broad and not aligned with its operating environ-ment. As IBRA's name indicates, it was originally envisioned to be a bank restruc-turing agency. But as the crisis deepened, it was assigned a number of other tasks that were not necessarily compatible or fully aligned with its operating environment. Each of these tasks (bank restructuring, corporate restructuring, and pursuing bank owners for misuse of liquidity support) was significant in its own right and in hindsight might have been better placed in separate institutions. Combining them all under IBRA's umbrella created an undue concentration of wealth in an environment of poor governance and oversight. It also created sequencing problems in that restructuring of banks had to take precedence and led to delays in asset disposition and pursuit of shareholders. And although the goal of restructuring loans and corporates may have been laudable, it signifi-cantly delayed the recognition of losses. Restructuring was simply not feasible given the sheer number of loans involved; the high concentration value in loans to a few politically well-connected borrowers; prolonged macroeconomic instability with high interest rates and exchange rate volatility, making it difficult to assess a borrower's debt service capacity; and total lack of support from the dysfunctional legal and judicial system.

Capacity building takes time and requires a dedicated institutional-strengthening program. AMCs are complex organizations that must become fully operational within relatively short periods; however, meaningful capacity building takes time. Unlike the SDIF, which adopted an institutional-strengthening program soon after it gained its independence, IBRA gave little thought to its internal organizational structure. This reflected not only the rapidly evolving nature of the crisis and IBRA's growing mandate but also the lack of proper oversight on the part of the board and the revolving occupation of the chairman's position. Managing IBRA became more difficult as operating units became self-contained silos with little central control or information sharing. Internal management reports lacked relevant information for decision making. Databases were lacking and risk management nonexistent. Although improvements were noted over time, IBRA would have benefited from greater attention in the early days to building a strong internal infrastructure that facilitated proper information sharing, risk management, and internal controls.

Danaharta, Malaysia

Context of the Creation of Danaharta

Danaharta was established in June 1998 as a preemptive tool to address rapidly growing NPLs in the banking system as a result of contagion from the Asian crisis. In 1997, GDP fell by 6.7 percent, the local currency depreciated by 50 percent against the dollar, and the Kuala Lumpur Composition Index dropped to half of its value. Although banking system NPLs (measured as over six months past due) had remained about 2–3 percent of total loans over May–September 1997, by August 1998 they had reached 11.5 percent.

Danaharta was one pillar of a comprehensive strategy to strengthen the banking system. The other pillars were Damodal, a fully owned subsidiary of Bank Negara Malaysia (BNM), responsible for capital injections into viable banks; a Corporate Debt Restructuring Committee (CDRC) to encourage voluntary out-of-court restructuring throughout the economy; and a merger program for banks, with the objective of merging the 21 domestic commercial banks, 25 finance companies, and 12 merchant banks into 6 core banks. A steering committee oversaw the coordination between Danaharta, Damodal, and the CDRC as well as their performance.

Mandate and Legal Powers

Although established as a corporation under the Companies Act, Danaharta was granted special powers to allow crucial activities to be carried out outside the court process. These powers included (i) the ability to buy assets through statutory vesting so that Danaharta could acquire assets with certainty of title and maximize their value; (ii) the ability to appoint special administrators to manage the affairs of distressed companies to allow corporate restructuring; and (iii) the ability to sell foreclosed assets by way of private treaty without going through the court process, which also required amendments to the National Land Code. Financial institutions could sell foreclosed properties only by public auction and had to obtain court orders to sell charged properties.

The law granted Danaharta a broad mandate to manage and dispose of assets and liabilities. All institutions licensed under the Banking and Financial Institution Act (banks, foreign subsidiaries, and finance companies) were eligible to participate. The law did not have a sunset clause; instead, the minister of finance was provided with the discretion to terminate the act if circumstances no longer required it.

The board had multisectoral representation and included government officials, private sector representatives, and two members from the international community. Board members were subject to fit and proper rules. Regarding transparency, the law required only that annual audited accounts be submitted to the minister.

Establishment and Early Years

The founding law did not include provisions on the eligible assets, the transfer price, or the financing of Danaharta. The corporation decided to focus on large, industrial loans above RM 5 million, which represented over 70 percent of the banking system's NPLs and between 2,000 and 3,000 accounts. This was considered a manageable number.

As Danaharta was established as a preemptive mechanism, asset transfer was not compulsory but relied on a willing-buyer, willing-seller basis. To encourage banks to sell their NPLs to Danaharta, BNM provided a combination of "sticks" and "carrots" including:

Sticks

- All banks being recapitalized by Damodal would have to sell their NPLs to Danaharta.
- Banking institutions with a gross NPL ratio exceeding 10 percent were required to sell all their eligible NPLs to Danaharta; otherwise they would have to write down the value of these loans to 80 percent of the price offered by Danaharta. Danaharta made only one offer for each NPL.

Carrots

- BNM allowed banking institutions to amortize losses resulting from the sale to Danaharta up to five years.
- Profit-sharing arrangements with selling institutions were set up as follows: Danaharta would share any surplus recovery (after deducting recovery and holding costs) from the sale of the loans or assets, with the selling institutions receiving 80 percent of the surplus.
- Danaharta's bonds had a zero risk weight for capital adequacy purposes.

Danaharta established standardized parameters to determine the market value of the loans purchased. For secured loans, the market value was 95 percent of the market value of the property determined by a new appraisal. If the loan was secured by shares, the value was determined on the basis of the market price or net intangible assets of the companies and adjusted for the level of control. For unsecured loans, the market value was 10 percent of the principal amount outstanding. This was an arbitrary figure (KAMCO used 3 percent).

Danaharta also played a receiver role. The government and BNM gave Danaharta some NPLs of two failed banks to manage on their behalf, while liabilities and good assets of these banks were merged into an acquiring bank. These managed NPLs were vested into the corporation, and no price was paid.

Funding was obtained through the government's initial capitalization and bond issues. The government provided seed funding of RM 3 billion (1 percent of 1998 GDP). Danaharta initially contemplated the issuance of an international bond guaranteed by the government, but the fall of the currency and downgrades of Malaysia's credit ratings made this option expensive. Instead, the corporation issued five-year zero coupon bonds at a discount to financial institutions to purchase NPLs, with an option to extend for another five years. This relieved pressure on cash flows and gave time to assess the most appropriate strategy to dispose of

NPLs. The implied yield decreased from 7.15 percent in November 1998 for the first issue to 5.16 percent in March 2000 for the last issue. The bonds were discountable at the central bank as collateral under the lender of last resort window. However, the secondary markets never developed, and interest rates kept falling, which increased the value of the bonds on the books of financial institutions.

The management approach for the NPLs depended on the viability of the borrower and the currency of the NPLs. Foreign currency loans and marketable securities extended to and issued by foreign companies were sold right away. Danaharta had no comparative advantage because they were outside its jurisdiction. They were sold in restricted tenders. Local currency loans whose borrower was deemed viable were financially restructured. Danaharta issued its own loan restructuring guidelines to help borrowers formulate a workout plan and shorten the time to restructure. For local currency loans whose borrower was deemed nonviable or uncooperative, Danaharta either foreclosed on the collateral or appointed a special administrator (73 groups of borrowers). One unusual method of disposal was the securitization of performing restructured loans to raise cash quickly. It was used only once on 1.2 percent of the portfolio, as Danaharta was raising enough cash to finance its operations. Figure 5.1 illustrates approaches for asset disposal.

Performance and Winding-up

Danaharta is generally considered as a success story. It stopped the increase in NPLs in the banking system, repaid all its bonds as of March 2005, was wound up after seven years in December 2005, and incurred a small loss for the government, on a cumulative basis. Upon closure, Danaharta transferred RM 1.72 billion of unrecovered assets to the Ministry of Finance (about 3.6 percent of the

Figure 5.1 Danaharta: Asset Management and Disposition

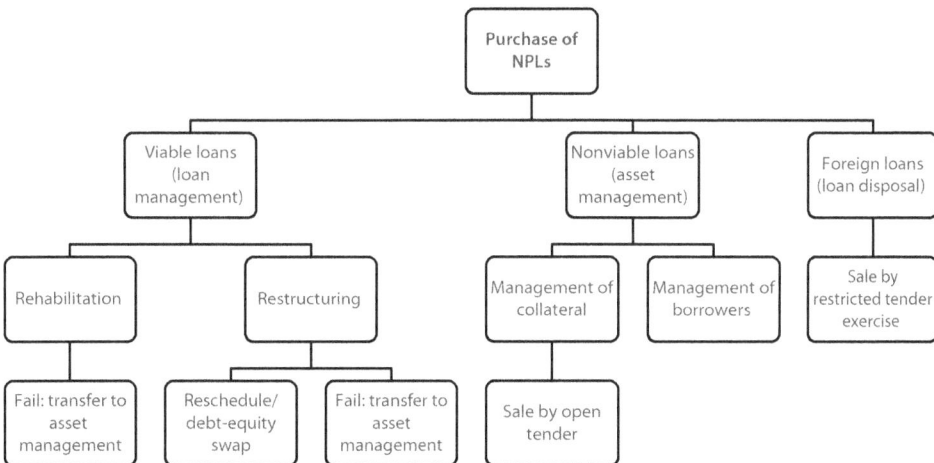

Source: Danaharta.

book value of managed and acquired NPLs). However, recovery figures were greatly improved by the "managed loans" that were not purchased by Danaharta and yielded a higher recovery rate than the purchased assets. This explained to some extent the limited use of the surplus sharing distribution. Without the income generated by the managed loans, Danaharta would have incurred a greater loss (it recovered only half of the adjusted value of purchased NPLs, which could suggest that the discount at purchase was not deep enough to recover a positive amount—table 5.10).

Lessons Learned

The success of Danaharta was due to a combination of factors. Three are highlighted below: the design factors, the economic environment, and the operations.

Design Factors

Danaharta was part of a comprehensive strategy to restore financial stability. It was one pillar of a comprehensive framework to restore financial stability and was complemented by a bank recapitalization agency, a voluntary loan workout agency, and a bank merger program. The actions of the three agencies were coordinated under a steering committee chaired by BNM.

Table 5.10 Danaharta's Key Figures

Key Indicators	
Equity capital (RM billion)	3
Face value of bonds issued to purchase NPLs (RM billion)	11
Bonds issued to purchase NPLs (1998–2000)	15
Companies with special administrators appointed by Danaharta	73
Property tenders in lifetime	25

Portfolio	RM billion	Simplified cumulative cash flow 09/2005	RM billion
Total NPLs	47.7	Total cash received from recovery proceeds	26.7
Including managed (from 2 banks)	28	Initial equity	3
Including acquired (from 70 institutions)	19.7	Borrowings	1.9
Number of accounts	2902	Other inflows including from placements	3
Average discount of acquired NPLs	54%	*Total cash inflows*	34.6
NPLs portfolio include accrued interests	52.4	Bond redemption	11.1
Managed NPLs	29.8	Surplus sharing distribution	0.8
Acquired NPLs	22.6	Recoveries from managed loans (net of fees)	15.6
Amount recovered during lifetime	30.4	Repayment of borrowings	2.1
Managed NPLs	19.3	Other outflows (include operational costs)	4.4
Acquired NPLs	11.1	*Total cash outflows*	34
Recovery rate	58%	Surplus	0.6
Managed NPLs	65%		
Acquired NPLs	49%	*Accumulated loss carry forward (P&L)*	−1.1

Source: Danaharta.
Note: NPL = nonperforming loans.

It had a clear mandate and enabling legal environment. Danaharta was granted special powers in its founding law to expedite the management of NPLs, and the national land code was amended to reflect such powers.

The response was systemic and preemptive. The structure of the banking system allowed Danaharta to perform a rapid clean-up while managing a limited number of loans. Danaharta carved out 70 percent of the financial system's NPLs with fewer than 3,000 loans (only 800 were acquired NPLs; the others came from the two failed banks). Most of these loans had been distressed for less than a year, which increased the chance of successful restructuring.

Economic Environment

Growth quickly resumed. Although growth was lower than before the crisis (GDP growth average of 4.3 percent in 1999–2005, versus 9.2 in 1991–97), the economy rebounded as early as 1999, which helped borrowers to stay afloat.

Capital controls may have helped corporates. There is a debate as to whether the imposition of capital controls in September 1998 helped Malaysia weather the crisis and protected its real sector. Unlike Korea and Thailand, Malaysia did not resort to promoting acquisition and takeover by foreign companies as part of the ongoing process of corporate and banking restructuring. An analysis of foreign direct investment (FDI) flows shows that net FDI flows remained broadly at the 1997 level in the three postcrisis years, rather than increasing steeply as in Korea and Thailand. In addition, Malaysia's foreign investment regime had remained much more liberal for a long time, and in some sectors, the presence of multinational enterprises had already reached very high levels by the onset of the crisis (Athukorala 2003). It seems instead that capital controls allowed room for lower interest rates, which made it easier for firms to repay or refinance their loans.

Operations

Danaharta showed strong corporate governance and transparency. Despite having few provisions in its founding law, Danaharta adopted a strong system of corporate governance. In 1999 its board published quantitative key performance indicator (KPIs) to assess Danaharta's effectiveness, with the objective of constantly beating the target. It adopted the Malaysian Code on Corporate Governance that was issued in March 2000. Danaharta published quarterly reports on its activities on its website. The board's tenure reflects stability and continuity.[17] No single individual was able to make decisions regarding the management of NPLs, as all key decisions were taken collegially in committees.

Staff incentives were implemented. Danaharta recruited experienced staff from the international and banking community. It outsourced legal, accounting, real estate, and marketing services so that the staff head count was kept lean (278 as compared with 334 permanent and 3,400 temporary staff for IBRA's asset management unit). Remuneration practices were benchmarked to local banks, and staff were rewarded on the basis of achievement of the KPIs.

Savings Deposit Insurance Fund (SDIF), Turkey

Context of the Use of the SDIF

From the early 1980s onward, Turkey experienced high and volatile inflation, an unsustainable buildup of public debt, and increasing financial fragility owing to poor economic policies and lack of fiscal discipline. Popular demands for higher wages and increased public spending led to fiscal imbalances and an accelerating rate of inflation, at the same time that interest rate deregulation and the shift from central bank financing to direct security issues raised the cost of financing public sector deficits. In response, the capital account was fully liberalized in 1989, effectively exposing the economy to international capital flows. The outcome was a substantial increase in the government's borrowing rate as the accelerating inflation rate raised the risk of holding assets denominated in Turkish lira. Public debt increased rapidly thereafter, in large part because of the need to finance the increased interest costs. The financial system became increasingly unstable due to large maturity mismatches and currency risks, as it relied on earnings from the long-term, high-rate government debt, financed by short-term, lower-rate international borrowing and domestic (including foreign exchange) deposits.

During the 1990s, Turkey experienced a series of sharp reversals in capital flows. The first occurred in 1991 after the Gulf War and was followed by another in 1994, triggered, in part, by the downgrading of the Turkish credit rating in international markets and efforts by the government to impose lower interest rates on banks participating in T-bill auctions. A deep but brief recession followed, with the economy recovering quickly as capital flows returned the following year. However, flows began to slow again following the onset of the East Asian crisis. The resulting decline in economic activity, together with the fallout from the Russian crisis and the devastating 1999 earthquake centered in Turkey's industrial heartland, combined to push the economy into a deep but short-lived recession.

These reversals culminated in the "twin crises" of 2000–01. In early November 2000, international banks began closing their interbank credit lines to Turkish banks as concerns about the Turkish economy and irregularities surfaced in several intervened banks. In late November, a private mid-sized bank's inability to finance the rollover of its bond portfolio prompted a sharp selloff of government debt and a rapid rise in interest rates, which briefly reached levels above 1,900 percent. The situation stabilized shortly thereafter with the announcement of an IMF program, but in February 2001 another, much more serious liquidity crisis began when tensions between the president and prime minister surfaced. Investors liquidated their positions; interest rates spiked as high as 6,200 percent; and the banking sector's already weak capital base was further eroded by interest rate losses, devaluation losses when the lira was allowed to float freely, and rising loan losses from the badly hit corporate sector.

Public Asset Management Companies • http://dx.doi.org/10.1596/978-1-4648-0874-6

Serious problems also began to surface in the banking sector, which had expanded rapidly throughout the 1990s.[18] The system was dominated by the four state banks, which held 40 percent of the system's assets.[19] In contrast, the private banks were weak and fragmented; most were part of financial conglomerates. Banks had come to depend upon high inflation and high interest rates as the government's financing needs had crowded out traditional lending[20] and dulled risk management skills, leading to an undue concentration of foreign exchange and maturity risk. NPLs rose sharply, peaking at 25 percent of total loans. Corporate distress was widespread, with nearly all sectors of the economy reporting steep declines in business activity, rapidly declining net profitability and major losses, and insufficient cash flow to meet expenses. Given that the private banks did not require public assistance and that the NPLs were not concentrated in easily managed assets such as real estate, the government chose to leave NPL restructuring in the hands of the banks. It did, however, undertake two initiatives to promote NPL restructuring (box 5.6).

Enhanced Powers and Operationalization

Turkey entered the crisis with an existing bank resolution entity modeled on the FDIC. Although deposit insurance was first introduced in Turkey in 1933, the SDIF itself was not formed until 1983. Its initial goal was to provide limited

---

Box 5.6 Initiatives to Promote NPL Restructuring

Although the government chose to leave nonperforming loans (NPL) restructuring in the hands of the private sector, it did promote two initiatives designed to accelerate restructuring efforts.

A quasi-formal workout procedure, known as the "Istanbul Approach," was introduced to expedite restructuring. It was based on the London Approach workout models adopted in Asia, particularly Korea. The Istanbul Approach, which encompassed commercial banks, financial intermediaries, Savings Deposit Insurance Fund (SDIF, Turkey) banks, and state banks, relied on a framework agreement that set forth the terms and conditions governing the restructuring of debt, including provisions allowing restructuring plans to be approved by a majority of creditors. As an incentive for banks and debtors to engage in restructuring, transactions (including new loans for working capital) restructured under the Istanbul Approach were exempt from a variety of taxes, duties, and fees. In effect from June 2002 to June 2005, the Istanbul Approach restructured over US$6 billion of debt for a total of 322 companies. Of this debt, 91.5 percent was restructured in the first year.

The formation of private AMCs was encouraged through the use of tax incentives. Five AMCs were established (most included participation by experienced foreign partners), and the SDIF took a small percentage of ownership in one to facilitate its sale of NPLs.

Source: World Bank (2010, 6–7).

---

deposit insurance and as such it operated as a "pay box" system. After the 1994 crisis, the deposit guarantee was expanded to cover all deposits and the SDIF was given responsibility for resolving failed banks. However, lacking the power to remove shareholders and effectively close banks, its resolution powers were weak and largely limited to the provision of liquidity support to illiquid but still solvent banks.

The SDIF was significantly strengthened by new legislation enacted in 1999.[21] Key provisions of the new law included the following:

Mandate:

- Retained the SDIF's dual mandate of administering the deposit guaranty scheme and resolving insolvent banks. The SDIF's previous role of liquidity provider to illiquid but still solvent banks was transferred to the Central Bank of Turkey (CBT).

Governance, transparency, and accountability:

- Removed the SDIF from the CBT and placed it under the Banking Supervisory Agency (BRSA), with clearly defined separation of roles between the BRSA and the SDIF.
- Provided for a seven-member board of directors, which included the BRSA's vice president.
- Required that the SDIF be included in the BRSA's annual independent audit and that the results, including any corrective actions or other measures taken, together with an annual report detailing BRSA and SDIF activities, be submitted to the Council of Ministers.

Enhanced resolution powers:

- Introduced the principle of least-cost resolution.
- Required the application of losses directly to shareholders' capital and the revocation of shareholders' rights.
- Expanded the available failure resolution techniques to include deposit transfer; purchase and assumption (including establishing a bridge bank or splitting the bank into "good" and "bad" banks); and depositor payoff.

Special Powers:

- Explicitly made majority shareholders responsible (later extended to managers by law No. 5411) for repayment of losses due to misuse of bank funds (liquidity support, legal lending violations, and the like).
- Enhanced the fund's recovery efforts by designating SDIF assets as "state receivables," thereby making them subject to Article 51 of Law 6183, Procedure for Recovery of Public Receivables. This entitled the fund to seize and sell debtor's assets regardless of whether they had been pledged to secure under-

lying debt through an administrative rather than civil procedure, thus considerably shortening the collection period.

The SDIF became an independent, autonomous agency in 2005. Although the majority of the provisions outlined above remained substantially unchanged, the new banking law, No. 5411, introduced the following provisions:

- Limited the period for bank resolution to nine months with one three-month extension allowed upon board approval.
- Stronger governance with the establishment of a seven-member board appointed by the Council of Ministers, criteria for appointment of board members, and provisions regarding minimum weekly board meetings and voting requirements.
- New mechanisms to ensure the exchange of information, cooperation, and coordination not only between the BRSA and the SDIF, but also among a broad range of other government institutions involved in ensuring the development and stability of the financial system.

The SDIF also faced a number of challenges in becoming fully operationalized. Although it had existed for a number of years, its newly expanded powers and responsibilities made it essentially a start-up operation. As such it faced a number of early challenges:

- A high volume of very poor-quality banks and nonperforming assets, the majority of which were connected to the majority shareholders
- A lack of secondary asset markets and an underdeveloped capital market, together with nonexistent investment banking practices and foreign direct investment, severely restricting funding for potential investors
- Lack of effective and efficient management practices for all asset classes
- Lack of expertise in bank restructuring and resolution
- Lack of experience in managing the outsourcing of legal collection work to a high number of regional practitioners.

Overcoming these challenges required the development and implementation of an institutional-strengthening program. Under the World Bank program, the SDIF adopted a time-bound institutional-strengthening program that resulted in (i) a more effective organizational structure, with clearly separated line responsibilities for bank resolution, asset management, and administration of the blanket guarantee and the deposit insurance scheme, together with supporting functions such as legal, human resources, and information technology; (ii) time-bound performance targets for bank resolution and asset disposition activities; (iii) appropriate staffing levels; and (iv) the installation of a centralized and high-quality management information system that allowed SDIF senior management and the board to monitor progress being made toward reaching agreed resolution and asset management and collection targets.

Funding

The SDIF was initially funded by borrowings (cash and/or securities) from the Treasury and CBT as well as its own funds. In addition to the use of paid-in deposit insurance premiums, the SDIF was granted the ability to require banks to prepay their insurance premiums in an amount not to exceed the amount paid in the previous year.

In mid-2008, the Treasury assumed the cost of the recapitalization program. The SDIF's debt (principal, interest, expenses, and default fines) to the Treasury was cancelled in recognition that the cost of the bank recapitalization program was more properly a burden of the state. The SDIF is required to remit to the Treasury the balance of all liquidation proceeds net of current and probable recovery expenses and other required payments such as taxes, social insurance, and other creditors.

Asset Disposition[22]

The SDIF was responsible for the managing the recovery efforts of three distinct types of assets. They were equity positions in the banks in which the SDIF intervened, NPLs (including shareholder obligations arising from violation of banking regulation), and miscellaneous bank assets (including subsidiaries) that were not included in sale transactions.

Banks

With the enactment of the amended banking law in December 1999, the SDIF began intervening in insolvent banks. From 1997 to late 1999, the SDIF had intervened in only three banks, with little progress toward their resolution. But, upon the enactment of the amended banking law in December 1999, the SDIF promptly intervened in five deeply insolvent banks and a sixth bank was placed in liquidation. Over the next two years, the SDIF would intervene in 11 additional banks, bringing the total number of banks under their control to 20 (approximately 20 percent of the sector).

In total, the resolution of the SDIF banks yielded over US$1 billion through the end of 2006. After it became fully operational, the SDIF moved quickly to remove nonperforming assets, recapitalize, and resolve its banks, employing a variety of methods. Of the 20 banks taken over, five were sold by an open and transparent sale process to three Turkish groups and two foreign banks, who paid US$352,624 million for 61 percent of the banks' balance sheets and assumed some US$2.4 billion in liabilities as well as approximately 8,000 staff members (BRSA 2003, 30). The remaining banks were either merged into other banks or liquidated. One bank, Bayinder (subsequently renamed Joint Fund Bank), has continued to operate as a transition bank conducting the "soft" liquidation of performing assets that required a banking license and off-balance sheet liabilities not included in the sale of the banks. By the end of 2006, Bayinder's efforts had yielded over US$1 billion. Resolution time for all banks, with the exception of Bayinder, ranged from 6 to 30 months, with an average resolution time frame of 14 months.

Table 5.11 Assets Transferred to SDIF

Type	Number of Assets	Approximate Book Value (US$ billion)	Cash Proceeds Realized (US$ billion)
NPLs, shareholders	1,437	5,000	9,591
NPLs, corporates	16,500	5,000	868
NPLs, personal loans	188,856	5,000	106
Total	**206,793**	**5,000**	**10,565**

Source: SDIF (2006, 23) and World Bank estimates.
Note: SDIF = Savings Deposit Insurance Fund (Turkey); NPLs = nonperforming loans.

Nonperforming Loans
By the end of 2006, the SDIF had recovered US$10.6 billion, 91 percent of which had come from the shareholder NPLs (in value; table 5.11). Over 200,000 NPLs with a book value of approximately US$5 billion were transferred to the SDIF as part of the bank recapitalization process. Of these loans, 91 percent consisted of small-value personal loans, with the balance consisting of corporate loans and shareholder receivables representing the sums owed on regular commercial loans as well as the repayment of funds that had been misused by the owners (which were far larger in volume than personal loans).

The SDIF's collection efforts were greatly enhanced by its ability to collect NPLs under the Public Receivables Act No. 6183. Although the SDIF used a variety of approaches to collect NPLs including restructuring (both directly and in participation with the Istanbul Approach), discounts for early payment of personal loans, portfolio sales, and legal proceedings for uncooperative borrowers, the bulk of the collections came from the shareholder receivables. The clear enunciation that majority shareholders were liable for the misuse of funds in the Banking Act, coupled with the designation of the resulting receivables as state assets subject to collection under the Public Receivables Act No. 6183, greatly facilitated the recovery of amounts well in excess of their stated book value. As state receivables, shareholder NPLs were not eligible for discounts or sale. Instead, long-term repayment agreements covering not only the sums owed but also interest, penalties, and fees were entered into. The SDIF's ability to seize assets not serving as collateral proved to be a powerful incentive for cooperation as well as a source of repayment.

In addition to its traditional collection activities, the SDIF conducted three loan sales. The first, in December 2003, was withdrawn when none of the eight proposals submitted met the SDIF's reserve price. Following this failed sale, the SDIF, with the assistance of a consultant, developed its own valuation methodology to assist in determining reserve pricing. The non-shareholder NPL portfolio was eventually sold in two tranches (table 5.12).

Other Assets
Sale of other assets raised US$1 billion. The SDIF raised US$465 million, more than twice the estimated book value, from the liquidation of some 5,000 pieces of real estate and movable property (74 percent of the portfolio). In addition,

Table 5.12 SDIF NPL Sales

Date	Loans	Book Value (US$ million)	Price (US$ million)	Recovery (%)
December 2003	279	324.2		Withdrawn
August 2004	281	223	22.5	10
Late 2005	+10,000	934	161	17[a]
Total		1,157	183.5	16

Source: Akdağ (2011), Managing Assets, SDIF Experience: slide 35.
Note: SDIF = Savings Deposit Insurance Fund (Turkey); NPLs = nonperforming loans.
a. Included 43 percent participation in future revenues, which amounted to an additional US$4.5 million by the end of 2006.

Table 5.13 Distribution of Gross Cash Revenues from Resolution Activities (US$ millions)

	End 2005	2006	End 2006
Gross cash revenue	6,459	6,890	13,349
NPLs	4,534	6,035	10,569
Subsidiaries	538	55	593
Real estate and movables	380	85	465
Banks	790	705	1,495
Other	217	10	227
Financial revenues	505	85	590
Total revenue	6,964	6,975	13,939
Repayment to treasury			6,454

Total revenue as share of 2000 GDP (%): –5.6 percent

Source: SDIF Annual Reports (2005, 2006).
Note: GDP = gross domestic product; SDIF = Savings Deposit Insurance Fund (Turkey); NPLs = nonperforming loans.

US$593 million was received from the sale or liquidation of 139 subsidiaries (70 percent of the portfolio).

As of December 31, 2006,[23] the SDIF had collected US$14 billion from its resolution activities and repaid US$6.5 billion (38 percent) of the US$17 billion borrowed from the Treasury, as well as US$2 billion in short-term borrowings from the Central Bank.[24] In fact, 2006 represented the high water mark in the SDIF's collection activity: the sums realized were greater than the total amount received during the preceding five years. The bulk of the collections (72 percent) came from the shareholder NPLs (tables 5.11 and 5.13).

Lessons Learned

The Turkish experience (like those of the United States and Korea) clearly demonstrates that asset management functions can be effectively performed by existing institutions. In those cases where an existing institution, such as a deposit insurance fund, is mandated to resolve banks and their assets, is sufficiently independent and protected from political interference, and possesses strong collection powers, a new agency need not be set up. The use of an existing agency also avoids prolonged start-up periods.

Keeping the illiquid and insolvent SDIF banks open pending resolution increased the cost of resolution. The government's policy decision to keep these banks open rather than promptly paying off depositors and closing them proved costly. Their large capital and liquidity shortages forced them to continuously borrow in the interbank market at very high interest rates, which made them particularly vulnerable to the effects of the twin crises. The impact of the resulting interest shock wiped out nearly all of the US$5.6 billion of capital injected into these banks shortly before the crisis. This lesson was reflected in the 2005 Banking Law, which capped the maximum time a bank could remain open under the SDIF to 12 months.

NPL resolution lagged because of the SDIF's mandate to resolve banks, as well as their nonperforming assets. It is possible that an entity focused solely on traditional asset activities could have conducted a timelier disposition process. The SDIF's bank restructuring mandate forced it to put its primary emphasis on resolving the banks as quickly as possible. Asset management activities initially were of secondary importance, as reflected by the low level of collections in the early years. Asset resolution activities did not begin in earnest until 2005, some four years after the crisis began, when the SDIF became an independent, autonomous agency and substantially strengthened its organizational structure to provide the needed focus on asset disposition.

An adequate bank resolution framework is a key success factor in an efficient asset management process. Turkey entered the crisis with an updated banking law that introduced the principle of least-cost resolution, provided an effective means for taking control of a failed institution, and greatly expanded the available failure resolution techniques. The effective use of these powers coupled with such innovations as NPL sales, the ability to collect receivables under the Public Collections Act, and the ability to control and sell operating commercial entities in payment of receivables all contributed substantially to the SDIF's success in recovering the costs of the banking crisis.

Development of a market-based valuation methodology for all types of assets is essential. The SDIF assumed NPLs and other nonperforming assets from its banks at book value. Although these assets had been valued and written down in accordance with regulatory standards, their valuations still were substantially above market values. After the failure of the first NPL sale, the SDIF moved quickly to establish a comprehensive market-based valuation methodology that allowed it to properly price and sell its assets.

Notes

1. He (2004, 10). Fung et al. (2004, 24) puts the government ownership at 95 percent, which likely takes into account the ownership stakes of Korea Development Bank (KDB) and other banks nationalized during the crisis.
2. Korea Asset Management Corporation (KAMCO) received a cash loan annually from the budget to use for paying interest on the bonds.

3. This issue, KAMCO's sole international issue, was considered an important milestone as it was the first time an Asian country (other than Japan) had accessed international markets. In addition, it diversified the international investor base, which until this time had typically been U.S. based, and attracted international capital into the distressed-asset market.

4. This date coincides closely with the termination date for asset acquisition.

5. The number of banks had increased rapidly from 101 at the time deregulation was introduced in 1988 to 238 at the onset of the crisis.

6. For a detailed discussion of the bank restructuring program, see Enoch et al. (2001).

7. Bank Andromeda, owned by one of President Soeharto's sons; Bank Industri, a principal shareholder of which was one of the president's daughters; and Bank Jakarta, controlled by the president's half-brother.

8. The remaining 10 banks (out of 50 problem banks) were already subject to a program of recapitalization under the central bank.

9. This was subsequently extended for an additional year to allow for the orderly wind-up of the institution.

10. As was the case in Turkey, Indonesian Bank Restructuring Authority (IBRA) was established as part of the Banking Law rather than by a specific act.

11. The transferred banks consisted of 50 private banks that had borrowed at least twice their capital from Bank Indonesia and the four state banks already under restructuring.

12. For instance, IBRA's first budget was disclosed on a net basis (total operating costs less recoveries), owing to concerns about revealing the true cost of the recovery efforts. Lack of clarity regarding the administration of the government guarantee program led to undue delays in payment of claims, causing some bank owners to seek "assistance" from well-connected parties in order to gain access to their funds. Concerns arose over the perceived "generous" restructuring terms granted to some of IBRA's largest borrowers. IBRA's first audit opinion was qualified, owing to the valuation of the assets at book rather than market value, as required by accounting principles.

13. Banks generally sold above book value.

14. Approximately US$40 billion at an exchange rate of Rp 8,500 to US$1.

15. Some 1,900 corporate debtors (1 percent of all debtors) held 80 percent of the portfolio in value. Seven of the top 20 were among the top 25 conglomerates in Indonesia and had been the owners of the nationalized banks. Several were also being pursued by IBRA's AMI Unit for the repayment of liquidity support that had been misused during the early stages of the crisis.

16. In its life span, IBRA reported to four presidents, two ministries (Finance and State-Owned Enterprises), and seven ministers, and had six chairmen.

17. Danaharta had three chairmen and managing directors in its seven years of existence and one managing director became chairman. Two nonexecutive directors remained in place for the whole life. Most of them had a tenure of two years and more.

18. Total system assets in absolute terms tripled from US$57.9 billion (39.2 percent GNP) in 1994 to US$156.4 billion (77.3 percent GNP) as of the end of 2000 (PFSAL Project Report, p. 15).

19. These banks also needed massive recapitalization and restructuring. The program, however, was not subject to Savings Deposit Insurance Fund (SDIF, Turkey) intervention and thus is not discussed in this paper.

20. By 1999, the government had become the single most important borrower in the domestic market, with total new debt issues by the government twice as great as total banking sector loans (Akyuz and Boratov 2002, 15).

21. There is no separate deposit insurance or SDIF law, as the legal framework is embedded in central and commercial bank legislation.

22. Unlike most AMCs, the SDIF has an unlimited life span. For the purposes of this paper, an evaluation date as of the end of 2006 has been chosen, to compare with similar AMCs.

23. The SDIF has continued its recovery efforts. Through the end of 2012, gross recoveries amounted to US$20.7 billion, 75 percent of which came from continuing collections of nonperforming loans (NPLs) (primarily shareholder NPLs). The fund also continues to recover proceeds from the sale of the NPL portfolio, with total recoveries now amounting to US$171 million or 18 percent of the book value of the portfolio.

24. The total cost of private bank recapitalization was US$22.5 billion (8.4 percent of 2000 GDP), of which the SDIF borrowed US$17.3 billion from the Treasury and funded US$5.2 billion from its internal resources.

CHAPTER 6

The Third Generation: NAMA, AMCON, and SAREB

National Asset Management Agency (NAMA), Ireland

Context of the Creation of NAMA

NAMA was set up in a context of a severe banking crisis. In the face of tumbling bank share prices, and the collapse of construction and property markets, the Irish government announced in late 2008 a blanket guarantee of all Irish bank liabilities amounting to €440 billion, or twice the annual gross domestic product (GDP).[1] This guarantee was based on the belief that banks needed temporary liquidity but were intrinsically solvent. Bank share prices continued to fall sharply in 2008, on the back of a deepening recession and a steady fall in property prices, and in December 2008, the government announced its intention to inject capital into the three largest Irish banks. Anglo Irish was nationalized in January 2009 in the face of continuing deposit outflows. In February 2009, the Irish government injected €3.5 billion in cash into both Allied Irish Banks and Bank of Ireland in return for preference shares. In March 2009, the report of the special adviser to the government (Peter Bacon) on options for resolving troubled property loans proposed the creation of NAMA.

The choice was between NAMA and an asset protection scheme similar to the one implemented at Citigroup, RBS, and ING at the time. Although such a scheme had the intuitive benefits of avoiding up-front costs to the government, limiting asset write-downs and thus recapitalization costs, the creation of NAMA was preferred for the following reasons (Bacon 2009):

- Property prices had not yet reached rock bottom. The banking crisis was fueled by a property boom and subsequent drop in property prices. Property-related lending of Irish credit institutions increased from 45 to over 60 percent of total credit between December 2002 and 2008. The proportion of "speculative construction and property lending" (where no construction or rental contract was in place) increased from 8 to 21 percent of total

construction and property lending between 2002 and 2007. It was thus critical to put a floor on the drop in property prices.

• The government needed to exit from the blanket guarantee. The asset protection scheme was similar to the blanket guarantee on banks' liabilities, for
which the government did not have any exit plan. As a result, the Irish sovereign debt was unfavorably priced, with sharp increases in the credit default
swap spread from mid-2008. An additional guarantee of banks' property-related loan assets would have further intertwined the sovereign rating with
Irish banks' capital adequacy problems, without providing any clarity as to
how capital adequacy would be achieved.

• To reestablish credibility in the Irish banking system, losses needed to be
crystallized on bank balance sheets. As regards loans acquired by NAMA
from the participating institutions, banks would not have been required to
measure them at fair value while they were still on their books. An asset
valuation would only have been carried out on a loan portfolio if it were
mooted for sale or transfer. Without NAMA, the participating institutions
would have measured their loan books in accordance with International Financial Reporting Standards (IFRS), specifically IAS 39. This accounting
mechanism requires loans originally arranged and advanced by the banks to
be measured on an amortized cost basis; this was done on the assumption
that the loans would remain on the institutions' books until maturity. The
NAMA acquisition model was designed to force the institutions to recognize
their losses earlier than their own IAS 39 accounting valuation methodology.
The concern of the authorities was that in the absence of NAMA, there
would have been a phased unveiling of losses over time, with a consequent
drip-drip effect in terms of capital needs, and a corrosive impact on the cred-
itworthiness of the sovereign. The NAMA process therefore was designed to
enable the Irish banking system to recognize and address up front its loan
loss difficulties.

• Doubt existed that the banks responsible for the crisis could effectively manage the troubled assets. The assets were not complex financial instruments,
whose resolution might be best undertaken by the originators, but "plain
vanilla" property assets (development land, work in progress, unsold residential stock, and so on). NAMA offered the benefits of creating economies of
scale in administering workouts, expediting loan resolution with specific expertise, and breaking "crony capitalist" connections between banks and developers.

• Property developers were unable to work out impaired assets. Irish developers were not publicly quoted and did not have access to capital markets to
work out the impaired assets. Many developers, in companies of all sizes, had
little or no supporting corporate infrastructure, poor governance, and inade-
quate financial controls. The banks had failed to ensure that Irish property
companies, to whom they advanced billions of euros in lending, operated according to sound corporate governance standards. NAMA was envisioned to

have the capacity to oversee project development and attract long-term capital in a manner that individual development companies could not.

Mandate and Legal Powers

NAMA was created by an Act of Parliament in November 2009 and established the following month. It had four statutory objectives:

- Acquire impaired assets from the credit institutions participating in the NAMA scheme.
- Deal expeditiously with the assets.
- Protect, or otherwise enhance their value, in the interests of the state.
- Insofar as possible and consistent with those purposes, obtain the best achievable financial return for the state.

NAMA was provided with limited special powers to facilitate its access to the underlying real estate collateral and realize the security. In practice, these powers were never used.

- Vesting orders and compulsory purchase orders. The right of NAMA to ask the Court for a vesting order enables it to avoid having to go through a fire sale for some underlying land assets. The compulsory right of purchase enables NAMA to acquire land assets in situations where debtors might try to frustrate the realization by NAMA of its own assets.
- Powers designed to address particular technical legal difficulties and issues peculiar to NAMA and its operations. In particular, this included the right to (i) receive information on a borrower from the tax authorities and (ii) be protected against potential claims from other creditors in cases where NAMA receives payments from an insolvent borrower in preference to and ahead of such other creditors.
- Power to appoint a statutory receiver on security for loans owned by NAMA, not subject to restriction in the legislation governing land sale.

To avoid consolidation in the Irish public accounts, NAMA established a special-purpose vehicle (SPV). The National Asset Management Agency Investment Limited (the Master SPV) is owned at 51 percent by three private companies and 49 percent by NAMA. The Master SPV purchases, manages, and sells the distressed assets and issues the debt securities to purchase assets. Under the shareholders' agreement between NAMA and the private investors, NAMA exercises a veto over decisions taken by the company.

Any credit institution was allowed to sell assets to NAMA, including subsidiaries of foreign banks. The act set out a period of 60 days for application. Five credit institutions elected to participate (68 percent of total banking assets), all covered by the blanket guarantee except Irish Life and Permanent (ILP).

Although the Bacon report recommended a mandatory approach to asset transfer, it was not in the end required in light of the significant public ownership of the Irish banking system.[2] Given the dire state of public finances, foreign banks were asked by the Irish government to resolve their capital deficiencies with their parent companies, before using public funds (through NAMA or recapitalization).

Eligible assets were focused on property loans. They included any other loans to a debtor (connected loans) as well as derivative instruments. NAMA was granted the discretion to choose whether to acquire an eligible asset.

Establishment and Early Years

NAMA moved expeditiously to purchase assets in nine months. By the end of 2010, almost all of the loans acquired from the participating banks had been transferred to NAMA. The minister of finance allowed NAMA to acquire some loans before the completion of due diligence at an interim price based on criteria set out by the minister and the board. This was intended to overcome deficiencies in the loan documentation that would have delayed asset purchases beyond 2011. Following subsequent completion of due diligence, the purchase price was adjusted, and the full valuation process completed in March 2012.

NAMA did not use an AQR to assess the transfer price. The values at which eligible bank assets were acquired were determined in accordance with regulations made by the minister of finance in March 2010, using a methodology approved by the European Commission. The discounted cash flow of the collateral values was used, and the NAMA discount rates were set down in the regulations. NAMA appointed real estate appraisers to value approximately 10,700 properties. In parallel and continuing after NAMA purchased the assets, the Central Bank of Ireland implemented two rounds of forward-looking capital requirements assessments, in 2010 and 2011. These exercises, together with the application of NAMA haircut resulted in cumulative capital requirements of €79 billion (46 percent of 2011 GDP).

NAMA adopted a long-term economic valuation methodology. It applied an uplift factor to reflect anticipated proceeds from the property sales when markets conditions normalized. The average uplift factor was 8.3 percent. NAMA adjusted the value for excess collateral and assumed that future enforcement and acquisition due diligence costs would reduce projected disposal receipts by 5.25 percent.

NAMA acquired over 12,000 loans at a cost of €31.8 billion from the five banks that participated in the NAMA scheme. The face value of the loans and associated financial derivatives acquired was €74.4 billion. This crystallized losses in the banks of €42.6 billion or 57 percent of the amount owed by borrowers.[3] Loans in excess of €20 million were transferred.[4] There was a plan to transfer smaller commercial real estate loans to NAMA, but the government in 2011 decided not to proceed. This would have resulted in the purchase of about 20,000 additional loans for a cost of €12 billion.

In hindsight, NAMA overpaid the financial institutions. Because of the long-term economic value uplift applied to the loans, NAMA overpaid by some

€5.6 billion. In addition, NAMA's acquired loans were valued by reference to a property collateral valuation date of 30 November 2009 and, as a result, NAMA had to absorb losses arising from the impact of the 25–30 percent decline in Irish property values that took place subsequently right up to the end of 2013 (an estimated €4.5 billion impact). It is estimated that NAMA overpaid the banks on the transaction date by about €10 billion.

Ultimately, NAMA acquired 90 percent of the identified eligible loans, and the major uncertainty regarding the value of these loans was removed from the books of the banks. It issued government-guaranteed bonds amounting to €30.2 billion to the banks to pay for the loans it acquired. The balance of 5 percent (€1.6 billion) was paid by the issue of subordinated debt. Payment of interest and value at redemption of the subordinated debt depend on NAMA's financial performance (the banks had to write off this portion, in accordance with central bank regulations). Loan acquisitions represented about 46 percent of the property-based lending held by the participating banks.[5]

Because NAMA acquired property debtor connections, it also acquired performing loans. About 20 percent of the loans were performing. In the early years, these were useful for providing cash to the fledging agency.

Performance

The ultimate measure of NAMA's performance is cash generation from its portfolio. This is the key to NAMA's ability to meet its ultimate objective of repaying its debt, the senior government-guaranteed bonds issued to the financial institutions, and its ability to invest in its assets so as to increase their long-term recoverable value. A key element has been NAMA's approach to managing its debtors. It manages directly the largest debtor relationships (191 debtors, representing 82 percent of the portfolio) and the rest are managed by the banks. Through this approach, it required all debtors to agree to business plans by the end of 2012, and the business platform created through this agreement has been an essential driver of NAMA's ability to generate both recurring income, mainly rental income from properties securing its loans, and sales income. Property sales up to the end of 2014 account for about 58 percent of the portfolio acquired. About 80 percent of the total cash generation stems from property sales; the remainder is derived from rental income from receivers and debtors (table 6.1).

NAMA adopted a consensual approach with its debtors. It is working consensually today with about 70 percent of its debtors. For debtors, this has meant

- Agreeing to schedules of asset and loan sales,
- Reversing certain asset transfers,
- Granting NAMA charges over unencumbered assets,
- Putting rental income from investment assets controlled by debtors within NAMA's control, with rents lodged to bank accounts over which NAMA has security. Before NAMA's acquisition of the loans, the banks had little visibility and less control over such income.

Table 6.1 Key Figures

Portfolio	
Total acquired portfolio (€ billion)	32
Loans	12,000
Debtors	780
Average discount of acquired NPLs (%)	57
Regional share of portfolio (%):	
Ireland	54
United Kingdom	34
Northern Ireland, United States, European Union	12
Asset type, share of portfolio (%):	
Land and development	29
Office, retail, hotel	54
Residential	17
Recoveries to end of 2014	
Cash generated (€ billion)	23.7
Assets sales (€ billion)	18.7
Redemption of senior bonds, share of total (%)	55

Source: NAMA, https://www.nama.ie/financial/key-financial-figures/
Note: NPL = nonperforming loan;

When a consensual approach has not been possible, NAMA has taken enforcement actions. About 456 insolvency appointments had been made up to the end of 2014, relating to 353 of the 780 debtor connections originally acquired.

Because of the declines in the value of the properties securing NAMA's loans, NAMA has had to impair its book further. Following completion of its 2014 impairment review, NAMA had recorded a cumulative impairment provision of €3.6 billion against its loans and receivables portfolio. However, the upturn in the Irish property market since the middle of 2013 led initially to a reduction in impairment, and it is expected that NAMA's results in 2015 will show a net reversal of impairment provisions recorded in earlier years for the first time.

A key feature of NAMA's work, particularly in Ireland, has been to provide funding on a commercial basis both to complete existing development projects and to commence new projects. NAMA has approved funding of €1.6 billion across a range of residential and commercial development projects in Ireland and has indicated that it could advance up to a further €3 billion for residential development and delivery of the Dublin Docklands Strategic Development Zone, a fast-track planning area earmarked to provide commercial accommodation for the growing foreign direct investment in Ireland.

Lessons Learned

NAMA's strong performance since inception can be explained by several factors.

It has a clear mandate with a commercial focus. NAMA's raison d'être is to get the best possible returns for the state and to do so expeditiously. This has driven the organization to sell in all instances where reasonable returns could be achieved.

NAMA benefits from transparency and independence. NAMA reports quarterly and its management reports to Parliament every six months. It is subject to an audit report on its performance at least every three years. Although NAMA is under high scrutiny, it has also been granted operational independence. Its management makes decisions on what and when to sell (under the act, it is a criminal offense to influence NAMA). Independence has allowed NAMA to resist pressure from purchasers to sell at fire sale prices and from debtors.

NAMA implemented swift asset purchases and its assets were concentrated. NAMA completed its asset purchases within a year of becoming operational, obtaining special dispensation to purchase assets before the completion of the due diligence so that the strategy for asset management could be implemented in a timely manner. About 25 percent of its debtors represented 82 percent of the debt acquired: this allowed efficiency in managing the assets.

NAMA benefitted from economic recovery and a good property mix. U.K. assets provided 80 percent of sales in 2010–12, and allowed the rapid generation of cash. Since 2013, the recovery in the Irish property markets has accelerated Irish asset disposals. NAMA actively initiated a program of asset sales by its debtors in the U.K. in the period from 2010 to 2012, when conditions were strong in that market. Likewise, it responded actively when conditions in the Irish market improved significantly in 2013 and 2014. That approach accords with two key principles underpinning NAMA's stated strategy: no fire sales and no hoarding. In each of its main markets, its approach has been to release assets for sale in a phased and orderly manner that is consistent with the level of demand, the availability of credit, and the absorption capacity of each market.

Another positive impact of NAMA has been to professionalize the real estate market in Ireland. The boom was partly originated by real estate companies with limited transparency. NAMA developed transparent processes and large package deals to attract more professional investors, such as private equity groups.

However, six years into existence, NAMA is facing challenges:

- The staffing is becoming a major challenge. NAMA started with 10 staff in January 2010 and grew to 369 at the end of the 2014. To remunerate staff at par with the private sector, NAMA implemented bonuses linked to cash generation. However, as NAMA was deemed to fall under the public sector pay policy in Ireland, bonuses have been eliminated and wage cuts applied. NAMA has lost critical staff as a result. This is a key issue for AMCs, which need to work themselves out of business. With the agreement of the Irish minister for finance, NAMA has introduced a modest retention scheme with redundancy payment if staff remain until the institution is wound up.

- The cleanup of the banking system: NAMA could not have cleaned up the bad assets of the banking system because the scale of bank difficulties extended beyond land and development loans. The level of nonperforming loans (NPLs) in the Irish banking system were still very high at the end of 2014 at 23 percent of total loans, as the banks retained SME loans, distressed mortgages, and—in the case of two of the participating institutions—smaller property loans. The difficulties that the banks have experienced in working out these classes of loans clearly illustrates both why it was necessary to establish a stand-alone AMC to deal with land and development loans in the first place and the need for complementary policies to deal with small NPLs such as a new personal insolvency framework and accelerated write-off policies.

Asset Management Corporation of Nigeria (AMCON), Nigeria

Context of the Creation of AMCON

The Nigerian financial system underwent major structural changes leading up to the 2009 crisis and beyond. In 2005, the Central Bank of Nigeria (CBN) mandated all banks to increase their paid-up capital from ₦2 billion to ₦25 billion to strengthen their efficiency and competitiveness. This led to a forced consolidation of the sector from 89 banks in 2005 to 24 by 2006. During this period, credit to the private sector expanded rapidly. Most of the funds were used to purchase stock ("the margin loans") in the same domestic commercial banks that were extending the credit. Banking system assets doubled from 2005 to 2008 to reach 42 percent of GDP. When the equity bubble burst, NPLs rose from 8 to 29 percent of total loans between June 2009 and June 2010. Ten banks were particularly hard hit because of their large exposure to equity-related loans. The crisis was triggered by a sharp fall in the highly inflated stock market.

A special examination in the autumn of 2009 of all banks by the CBN and the Nigeria Deposit Insurance Corporation (NDIC) revealed that 10 banks were either insolvent or undercapitalized. Together, they represented one-third of the banking system. In addition to capital deficiencies, the banks were found to have serious deficiencies in liquidity, asset quality, risk management practices, and corporate governance. The NPLs were at 65 percent of total loans in these banks. The 10 banks were required to shore up their capital bases, and CBN replaced the management of eight of them.

The authorities intervened decisively by injecting liquidity into the troubled banks and providing broad guarantees. The CBN injected ₦620 billion (about US$4.1 billion) of liquidity into the banking sector in the form of unsecured and subordinated debt and provided a guarantee of all interbank lending transactions (expired at the end of December 2011), foreign credit lines, and pension deposits. The authorities made a public commitment to protect depositors and creditors against losses and announced that no bank would be allowed to fail. This ultimately entailed the protection of shareholders.

The need to act quickly and the shortfalls of existing resolution tools led to the creation of AMCON. The 10 banks had about ₦4.4 trillion of deposits (11 percent of GDP and 40 percent of the system's deposits), up to 10 million customers, and 50,000 staff. The NDIC had the powers under the Banks and Financial Institutions Act to restructure and resolve banks, and to manage the assets of a failing bank. However, these powers were subject to legal challenges, and the NDIC had to apply to the High Court to wind up a failed bank. Significant shortfalls that would impede the recovery of NPLs were also identified in the bankruptcy act. In addition, mobilizing public funds to inject equity into the banks would have required parliamentary approval, a processed considered more time-consuming than the creation of a new entity with this role. The challenges of the NDIC, combined with the need to act expeditiously to absorb the capital shortfalls of banks, and the vast amount of NPLs in the failed banks, led to the idea that an AMC with special powers would be the most appropriate tool to restructure these banks and recoup a portion of the cost. In July 2010, Parliament passed the act establishing AMCON. AMCON is a public corporation, fully owned by the federal government and the Ministry of Finance.

Mandate and Legal Powers

AMCON's mandate goes beyond that of a traditional asset management company and includes the capacity to recapitalize banks. The AMCON act provides the usual powers attributed to an AMC to manage assets, including the power to appoint a special administrator to facilitate corporate restructuring as in the act empowering Danaharta. However, the legislation also allows AMCON to invest in eligible equities subject to the approval of the CBN. Eligible equities are not defined in the act or in the guidelines, and do not seem to be restricted to the equity of financial institutions. Financial institutions whose assets may be acquired and/or managed by AMCON are all banks licensed by the CBN and those whose license has been revoked. In practice, the bank recapitalization mandate has dominated AMCON's role.

The legislation does not have any sunset clause. It caps the maturity of the bonds issued to purchase eligible assets to seven years but allows the CBN to change it. Nonetheless, the law caps the period for purchasing assets at three years and three months from the designation of eligible assets.

The CBN is granted significant powers over AMCON. It is designated as the regulator with the right to carry out examinations. Among other things, it determines the transfer valuation guidelines, the applicable accounting standards, the types of eligible bank assets and equity investments, and the tenure of the bonds issued by AMCON. It also has significant powers over the management as it appoints the chief executive officer (CEO) of AMCON, and 6 of the 10 board members. With ₦50 billion, it is the single most important contributor to the Banking Sector Resolution Cost Fund, established as a sinking fund to allow the bond redemption. This raises questions as to the independence of AMCON from its supervisor and creates conflicts of interest for the CBN (as the bank supervisor, it establishes standards for loans classification and provisioning; it has the power to select eligible assets to be transferred to AMCON, while being a shareholder and the supervisor of AMCON).

The act spelled out some governance and transparency safeguards but does not include financial safeguards. Board members should have at least 10 years of relevant experience, have no conflict of interest with AMCON's business, and disclose debt obligations and interest.[6] AMCON must submit an annual report to the Ministry of Finance and the CBN, and quarterly reports to Parliament, and publish its annual accounts. However, the act does not include any financial safeguards to limit the liability of the government as a shareholder. There are no provisions to limit the amount of assets or equity that AMCON may purchase or the bonds to be issued, no leverage ratio, and no requirement to maintain a minimum amount o equity.

The transfer price for eligible bank assets is to be determined in accordance with guidelines issued by the CBN, but there is no such provision for investment in equities. The act does not mandate for a comprehensive assessment (an AQR) of eligible financial institutions to be conducted before the transfer. It requires the CBN to be guided by independent advice when prescribing parameters for the valuation and to publish such parameters widely.

AMCON was thinly capitalized, in accordance with its act. The authorized capital was ₦10 billion, as compared with the approximately ₦2 trillion of NPLs (29 percent of total loans) at their peak in June 2010. As AMCON issued zero coupon bonds, initial capital was not needed to pay annual interest cost on the bonds but was intended to provide a buffer to cover operating expenses and absorb any operating losses, including impairment on acquired assets. If necessary, the capital may be increased upon recommendation of the board and the CBN board, and AMCON may borrow. Eligible assets are set to be purchased with the issuance of zero coupon bonds guaranteed by the federal government, discountable at the CBN, and investable assets for pension funds.

Establishment and Performance

AMCON moved expeditiously to purchase eligible assets (figure 6.1). Established in fall 2010, it purchased its first tranche of eligible assets of ₦866 billion in December that year. The speed can be explained by the nature of the assets. AMCON purchased about 12,000 loans—mainly in December 2010 and in

Figure 6.1 AMCON's Purchases

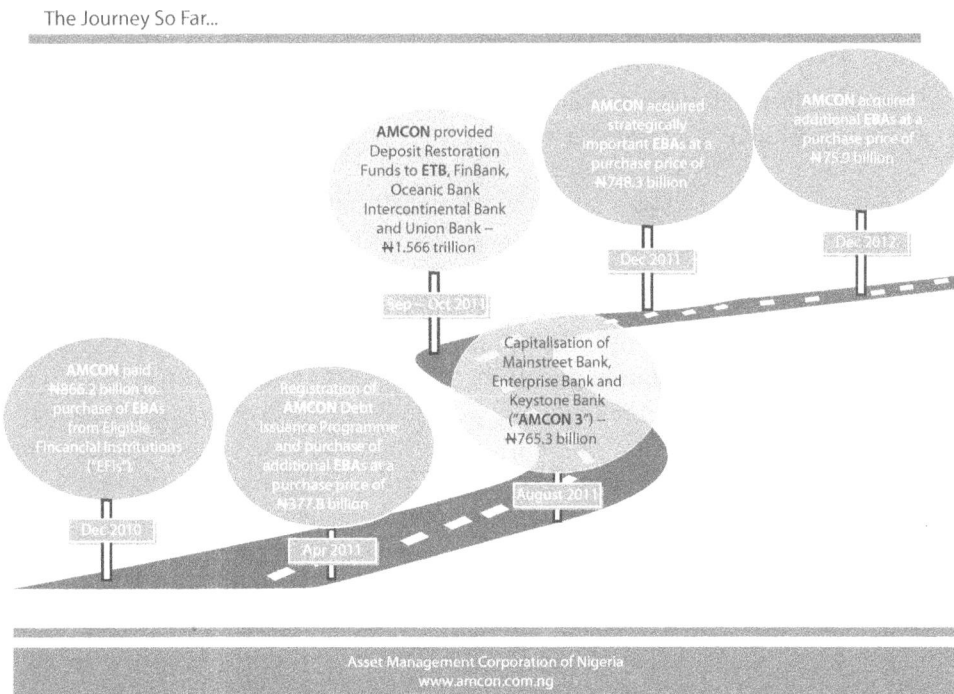

The Journey So Far...

AMCON provided Deposit Restoration Funds to ETB, FinBank, Oceanic Bank Intercontinental Bank and Union Bank – ₦1.566 trillion

AMCON acquired strategically important EBAs at a purchase price of ₦748.3 billion

AMCON acquired additional EBAs at a purchase price of ₦75.9 billion

Dec 2011

Dec 2012

Sep – Oct 2011

AMCON paid ₦866.2 billion to purchase of EBAs from Eligible Financial Institutions ("EFIs")

Registration of AMCON Debt Issuance Programme and purchase of additional EBAs at a purchase price of ₦377.8 billion

Capitalisation of Mainstreet Bank, Enterprise Bank and Keystone Bank ("AMCON 3") – ₦765.3 billion

Dec 2010

Apr 2011

August 2011

Asset Management Corporation of Nigeria
www.amcon.com.ng

Source: AMCON Roadshow (2013), website.
Note: AMCON = Asset Management Corporation of Nigeria.

Table 6.2 AMCON's Purchased Loans

Loan Distribution	% of AMCON Portfolio	Number of Loans
Combination of Assets	13	103
Debentures	15	295
Mortgage	20	2,096
Others	6	795
Shares	22	4,105
Shares & Mortgage	4	20
Unsecured	22	5,123
Total	**100**	**12,537**

Source: AMCON website.
Note: AMCON = Asset Management Corporation of Nigeria.

2011—for a consideration of about ₦2 trillion.[7] About 75 percent of the assets in number (45 percent in value) did not require physical real estate appraisals as they were secured by shares (the margin loans) or were unsecured. The CBN valuation guideline mandated that margin loans be valued at the greater of 5 percent of the principal sum or the 60-day moving average price of the underlying securities from November 15, 2010, plus a 60 percent premium; unsecured loans were to be valued at 5 percent of the principal. With only 20 percent of loans secured by mortgages, AMCON's portfolio looks very different from those of NAMA and SAREB (table 6.2).

Although the transfer was voluntary, in accordance with AMCON's act, the CBN provided strong regulatory incentives to ensure a massive transfer. The AMCON guidelines mandated that three months from its entry into force, eligible financial institutions should have no more than 5 percent of NPLs on their books. This was very effective, as the NPL rate decreased to 5.8 percent in December 2010. With such a massive transfer of assets, it is not clear that AMCON exercised its power to select the assets purchased on the basis of their recoverability.

AMCON most likely overpaid for eligible assets. AMCON claims that the average purchase price of eligible assets was about 45 percent, which is comparable to the average price NAMA paid [see the Financial Sector Assessment Program (FSAP) Technical Note, WB 2013]. However, the margin loans were purchased at a high premium: a 60 percent premium would have brought the value back to the peak of the all-share index in March 2008. Audited accounts show significant write-downs subsequently.[8] No data are publicly available on the discount AMCON applied to the different classes of eligible assets.

The interpretation of "eligible assets" led AMCON to purchase large performing loans and extend its portfolio. In the ₦2 trillion it paid, about ₦750 billion were strategically important eligible assets which were not necessarily NPLs.[9] For instance, in December 2011, with the CBN's agreement, AMCON purchased largely performing loans in the oil and gas sector from commercial banks for about ₦275 billion, paying between 85 and 95 percent of face value simply

Table 6.3 Distribution of Purchased Loans

Loan Distribution	% of AMCON Portfolio	Number of Loans
>N10b	40	62
N1b<loan< N10b	37	431
<N100m<loan< N1b	16	1,998
<N100m	7	10,046
Total	**100**	**12,537**

Source: AMCON website.
Note: AMCON = Asset Management Corporation of Nigeria.

because these loans were systemically important. This was seen as a political gesture because one of the debtors was owned by the minister of power.[10] The 62 large loans (strategic assets) represent 40 percent of the portfolio (table 6.3). A similar situation occurred for eligible equities, as AMCON fully purchased in 2011 a discount house that did not have any deposits; in addition, its balance sheet shows equity investments into an airline and a carmaker.

In addition to purchasing eligible assets, AMCON absorbed the negative equity of failed banks. Two of the 10 problem banks were recapitalized by their shareholders. For the other eight, AMCON absorbed the negative equity. This role was seen as critical to maintain financial stability but resulted in AMCON absorbing losses instead of shareholders, creditors, and depositors.

- AMCON provided fresh capital of about ₦1.56 trillion to five banks in which it intervened to bring them to zero net asset value. Subsequently, the injection of additional capital to ensure compliance with regulatory requirements was left to private investors.[11] Shareholders' interests were diluted but they were not written off completely even though the banks were insolvent. AMCON de facto absorbed the negative equity in these banks and allegedly received some equity for the capital injected. Although this measure was seen as necessary to prevent bank failures and depositor losses, AMCON is unlikely to recover from the transactions.[12]
- AMCON restructured and fully recapitalized three problem banks for about ₦765 billion. Spring Bank Plc, Bank PHB Plc, and Afribank Nigeria Plc were assessed as not being able to recapitalize before the CBN deadline of September 2011. The CBN revoked their licenses, and the NDIC incorporated three bridge banks—Enterprise Bank (for Spring Bank); Keystone Bank (for Bank PHB); and Mainstreet Bank (for Afribank Nigeria)—to assume the deposit liabilities and certain other liabilities, and the assets of the closed banks. AMCON purchased the equity of the bridge banks and injected capital up to the statutory minimum. AMCON absorbed the negative equity as well as any future loss in value. Mainstreet and Enterprise were sold in October 2014, with respective recovery of 42 and 32 percent of the relative investment (relative to the 25 percent target).[13] As of September 2015, Keystone remained to be sold.

The role of loss absorption and the overpayment for banks' eligible assets resulted in a massive negative equity position for AMCON. The 2014 audited accounts show an accumulated negative equity of ₦3.6 trillion (4 percent of 2014 GDP) compared with assets of ₦1.5 trillion. AMCON's ₦3.5 trillion debt was initially designed to be paid first from the proceeds of asset sales, with any remaining balance to be repaid out of the Banking Sector Resolution Cost Fund, to which Nigerian banks contribute yearly 0.5 percent of total assets, and the CBN's ₦50 billion contribution.[14] In 2013, in recognition of AMCON's inability to pay its debt, the CBN redeemed and refinanced AMCON's bonds. Repayment of the recapitalization costs is now a matter for the CBN and potentially a fiscal issue.

Information to assess the efficiency of the asset management function is scarce. The various reports mandated in the AMCON Act are not readily available, and no information is available on the performance of AMCON to recover on the assets purchased. Likewise, there is no information on recovery strategies and servicing arrangements. The audited accounts do not provide information on the income or cash recovered from the sale of loans or properties, as opposed to NAMA or SAREB. This may be due to a late start of the sale only four years after inception, and the need to focus on the resolution of the banks. Reportedly, AMCON has a policy of holding the real estate assets for at least three years before disposing the collateral.

Lessons Learned

AMCON's case shows that the role of AMC can be interpreted in various ways. Overall, AMCON's actions resulted in a cleanup and stabilization of the banking system. As of December 2014, the baseline CAR was 17 percent and the NPL ratio below 3 percent. However, the negative equity losses were transferred into the AMC with no expectation of recovery, rather than being allocated to banks' shareholders, depositors, and creditors.[15] AMCON's function was to bail out the banks as much as it was to manage the distressed assets, so as to prevent the liquidation of banks in a context of crisis. It was not created with the intention of limiting the overall fiscal contingent liability arising from the banking crisis.

Transparency about who shoulders the cost of resolution is important, to protect the AMC. It is difficult to allocate the costs of the resolution between AMCON and the CBN, and ultimately the banks. Although the intent of the Banking Sector Resolution Cost Fund is to recover the cost of resolving the banks from the banking sector, it will be some time before contributions matches the losses booked in AMCON. Though AMCON and the CBN are consolidated within the public accounts, the financial links between the two blur the ultimate accountability and responsibility for shouldering the cost of the resolution. This gives the impression that AMCON was created to hide losses arising out of the resolution.

Independence and appropriate governance are key success factors to ensure an AMC sticks to its mandate. The CBN has significant powers over AMCON as the mandate setter (defining assets and equities to be purchased), regulator, and creditor. These powers create conflicts of interest with the supervisory role of the central bank and may compromise its mission of attaining financial stability. AMCON's governance structure places its management under the influence of the CBN. The experience of other AMCs shows that those with effective independence have performed better.

A sunset clause is critical to focus the mandate of an AMC and protect the public purse. AMCON does not have a sunset clause. This increases the risk of mission creep, whereby AMCON may be called upon to avoid the failure of any financial or commercial entity, thereby increasing the cost for taxpayers. The absence of a sunset clause may also explain the lack of speed toward asset resolution, as compared, for instance, with NAMA.

A thorough diagnostic of the nature of NPLs should be done prior to setting up an AMC. In a crisis there may not be time for such a diagnostic; however, the nature of the NPLs will determine the need for an AMC and the design thereof. With insight, AMCON's loan portfolio raises questions about the need for an AMC with 44 percent of its loans secured by shares or unsecured, which do not require active management.

Sociedad de Gestión de Activos Procedentes de la Reestructuración Bancaria (SAREB), Spain

Context of the Creation of SAREB

Spain's real estate bubble burst after a decade of excessive leveraging. Construction and real estate loans grew from 10 percent of GDP in 1992 to 43 percent in 2009. Spanish banks were large relative to the economy: assets and loans were 227 percent and 172 percent of GDP in 2009. They funded their increasing exposures largely from external sources during the period of high global liquidity and low interest rates, rather than through the mobilization of savings. The freezing of wholesale markets and the onset of the euro-area debt crisis pushed the economy into a sharp recession by the end of 2008. In 2009, the economy contracted by 3.5 percent.

The authorities responded by providing liquidity support and initiating a vast program of consolidation in the savings banks. The deposit insurance limit was raised to €100,000 in October 2008, and the authorities implemented various guarantee programs of bank senior bond issues (€157 billion allocated over 2008–09). At the same time, the belief that the crisis was caused by inefficiencies in the savings banks led to the creation of the Fondo de Reestructuración Ordenada Bancaria (FROB) in 2009, as a public vehicle to restructure, recapitalize, and consolidate the banking sector. Between 2009 and 2012, the number of savings institutions was reduced from 45 to 11, through a combined set of actions including interventions, mergers, and takeovers. Mergers did not facilitate the recognition of problems since each party (acquirer and acquiree) had an incentive to improve the looks of their balance sheets.

The continuing deterioration of the economy unveiled increasing risks in real estate exposures and potential capital shortfalls in banks. Over 2010–11, NPLs to real estate developers jumped from 14 to 21 percent (figures 6.2 and 6.3). However, these loans had not been correctly provisioned, masking potential capital shortfalls. Although various initiatives to enhance the transparency of loan books and the recognition of losses were implemented (European Banking Authority Stress test, increased provisions on real estate exposures[16]), they were not sufficient to restore investors' confidence in the banking system.

The authorities thus resorted to a comprehensive bank restructuring strategy in 2012 including diagnostics, asset segregation, and restructuring and recapitalization. The strategy was adopted in the context of EU- and IMF-funded programs, which included various conditionalities to restore financial stability. One pillar of the strategy was the creation of the Sociedad de Gestión de Activos Procedentes de la Reestructuración Bancaria (SAREB) as a last-resort tool. At the time, there was no support from the main stakeholders for the creation of an AMC: the incoming government in 2012 had campaigned against it, the financial institutions did not want a fire sale of assets, and the real estate sector wanted a "bail-in."

Figure 6.2 NPL Ratios, 2008–11

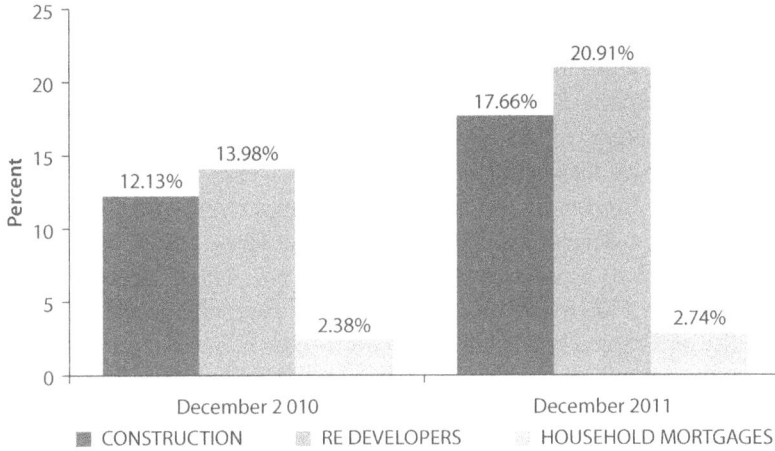

Source: BoS and SAREB.
Note: NPL = nonperforming loan; SAREB = Sociedad de Gestión de Activos Procedentes de la Reestructuración Bancaria.

Figure 6.3 Property-Related NPL Ratio

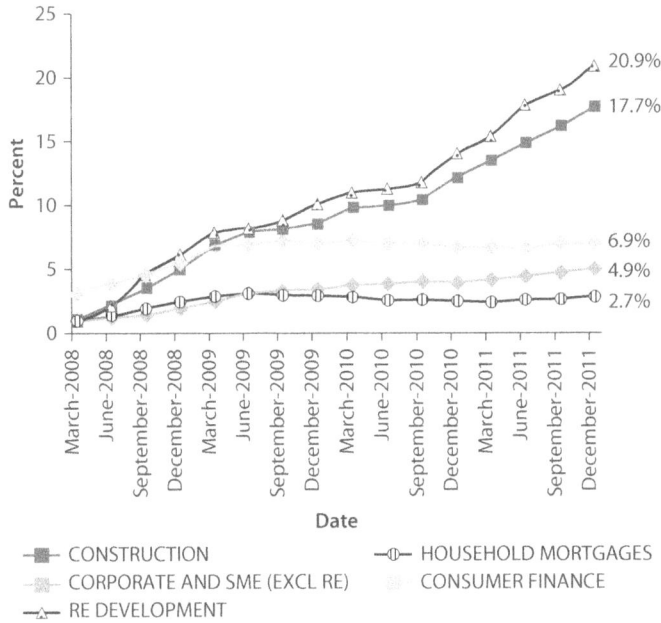

Source: BoS and SAREB.

Mandate and Legal Powers

The creation of SAREB was part of the July 2012 Memorandum of Understanding on Financial Sector Policy Conditionality[17] (MoU), signed between the European Commission (EC) and the Spanish government. The MoU provided external financing to Spain of up to €100 billion, of which only €41.4 billion was used (€38.9 billion for bank recapitalization and €2.5 billion for the capitalization of SAREB). Spain successfully exited the program in January 2014 (Directorate General for Economic and Financial Affairs 2014). SAREB was incorporated in November 2012, under the action of the FROB and in accordance with Law 9/2012, as a private company.[18] As with NAMA, the purpose was to avoid consolidating SAREB into public accounts.

SAREB's objective consists of the acquisition, management, and disposal of the assets that are transferred by credit institutions. These assets are legally defined in Ley 9/2012: (Disposición Adicional Novena). Those already under majority control of the FROB and those that, after an independent valuation of their asset quality and capital needs, the BoS deems to be in need of a restructuring or resolution process.

SAREB was created as private for-profit company with a public mandate. It did not have special legal powers, owing in part to its incorporation as a private company. Its founding decree specified the following mandate: (i) optimize the preservation and recovery of value, (ii) minimize possible market disruption that may derive from its activities, (iii) use capital efficiently, and (iv) be a for-profit company and therefore minimize the use of public funds and cost to the taxpayers.

SAREB's life span was defined by market conditions. The steep and continuous decrease in land and housing transactions since 2004 (figure 6.4) led to the establishment a life span of 15 years. This lengthy life span was deemed necessary to ensure a recovery of market prices in light of the volume of assets managed.

Design choices were driven by the necessity to take a definitive step to restructure and clean up the banks (figure 6.5). In the second half of 2012, the focus was on recognizing the losses at fair value, carving out the largest real estate exposures, and recapitalizing banks so as to limit the impact of further economic

Figure 6.4 Evolution of Housing and Land Transactions, 2006–13

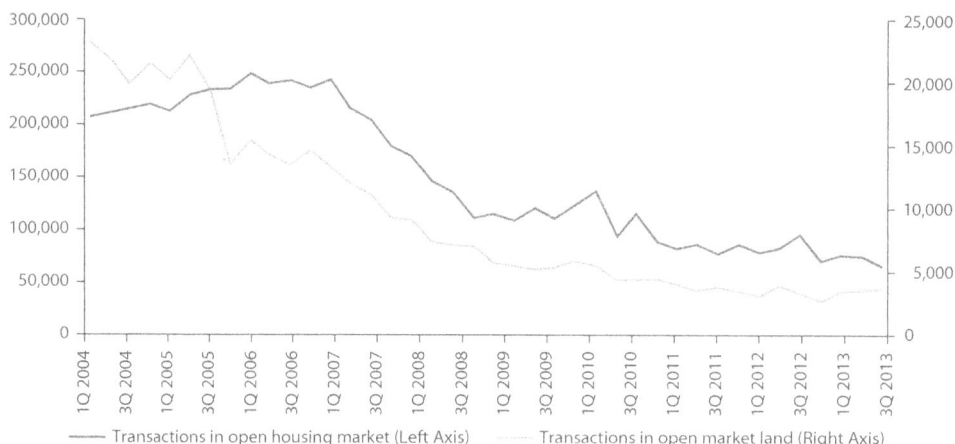

Transactions in open housing market (Left Axis)   Transactions in open market land (Right Axis)

Source: Spanish Development Ministry and SAREB.
Note: SAREB = Sociedad de Gestión de Activos Procedentes de la Reestructuración Bancaria.

Figure 6.5 Design Options for the Creation of SAREB

Questions	Choice	Rationale
① Public vs Private AMC	① Majority of private investors in capital and subordinated debt	① Avoid consolidation in public sector accounts; alignment of incentives
② Pooled AMC vs individual AMCs	② Single AMC for all banks receiving public financial support	② Ensure economies of scale; pool expertise; create distressed asset markets.
③ Compulsory vs voluntary participaion in AMC	③ Compulsory and restricted to banks receiving public financial support	③ Ensure sufficient participation
④ Market funding vs private funding	④ Private funding by transferors	④ Difficult to raise market funding at the time
⑤ Contingent vs defined valuation	⑤ Defined valuation at transfer	⑤ Asset Quality Review was done, allowing for an expeditious transfer of the assets

Source: SAREB and authors' analysis.
Note: SAREB = Sociedad de Gestión de Activos Procedentes de la Reestructuración Bancaria.

deterioration. This explained choices such as a single AMC, mandatory transfer, and defined valuation at transfer.

SAREB was one pillar of a comprehensive bank restructuring strategy. The strategy included the following elements, as defined in the MoU:

- A diagnostic to identify individual bank capital needs through an AQR and valuation process, as well as individual stress tests.
- Segregation into SAREB of the impaired assets of banks receiving public support.
- The recapitalization and restructuring of viable banks. Nonviable banks were resolved in an orderly manner. Banks receiving public capital had to allocate losses to holders of hybrid capital and subordinated debt (in many cases retail investors), in addition to equity holders.
- Bank regulation and supervision, together with the governance structure of savings banks and consumer protection were strengthened.

SAREB's governance structure followed that of private companies. It included a board of directors composed of 5–15 members, with at least a third of them being independent, and with six supporting committees. It is supervised by three entities:

- The BoS is responsible for supervising SAREB's compliance in three domains: (i) purpose, (ii) specific requirements regarding the transfer of assets, and (iii) rules guiding SAREB's governing bodies (in terms of transparency, creation, composition, and business behavior).
- The Securities and Exchange Commission (CNMV in its Spanish abbreviation) is responsible for supervising SAREB as an issuer of fixed-income securities.
- A commission composed of members from the Ministry of Economy, the Ministry of Finance, the BoS, and the CNMV monitors SAREB's performance against its objectives as an AMC, as well as the business plan.

Establishment and Early Years
Asset Valuation and Transfer

The transfer of assets from eligible banks was mandatory, so as to avoid adverse selection risks. As a result of the diagnostic, banks were allocated to four groups: (i) group 0: banks with no capital shortfall and where no additional actions are necessary, (ii) group 1: banks that were already owned by the FROB (five entities[19]), (iii) group 2: banks with capital shortfalls and unable to meet them without resorting to state aid (four entities[20]), (iv) group 3: banks with capital shortfalls that are able to enact recapitalization plans without resorting to state aid. The banks in groups 1 and 2 had to transfer all eligible assets to SAREB.

Only certain types of assets were eligible for transfer: loans with a net book value above €250,000, foreclosed properties with a net book value above €100,000, and other loans and properties originating from firms in real estate over which the eligible bank had control.

The asset valuation and transfer price were an average defined by the BoS, on the basis of valuation reports performed by independent experts. The assets were transferred to SAREB after the application of a discount rate that varied according to asset type (table 6.4). The average discount rate for the whole portfolio of assets transferred was 52.4 percent—about 63 percent for real estate assets and 45 percent for loans.

Overall SAREB received €50.8 billion of the market value of assets (5 percent of GDP), corresponding to 198,211 assets (table 6.5). This represented about 40 percent in value of the real estate assets owned by banks before the creation of SAREB. The number of assets received was much higher than in other AMCs (12,000 for NAMA and 3,000 for Securum and Danaharta). Financial assets or

Table 6.4 Average Discount Factor Applied to SAREB Assets

Average discounts (%)	
Financial Assets	
Completed housing	32.40
Projects under construction	40.30
Urban land	53.60
Other land	56.60
Other guarantee	33.80
No guarantee	67.60

Average discounts (%)	
Real Estate Assets	
New build housing	54.20
Projects under construction	63.20
Land	79.50

Source: SAREB (2013).
Note: SAREB = Sociedad de Gestión de Activos Procedentes de la Reestructuración Bancaria.

Table 6.5 Amount and Number of Assets Transferred to SAREB, by Type

Amount of assets (Millions of euros)	Group 1	Group 2	Total amount	% Total
Total gross assets	78,836	27,744	106,580	--
Total net assets	36,695	14,087	50,781	100.0
of which: loans/financial	28,299	11,140	39,439	77.7
of which: real estate	8,396	2,947	11,344	22.3
Implicit haircut	53.5%	49.2%	52.4%	--
Number of assets	Group 1	Group 2	Total amount	% Total
Loans/financial	68,149	22,616	90,765	45.8
Real estate	77,034	30,412	107,446	54.2
Total	**145183**	**53028**	**198211**	**100.0**

Source: SAREB (2013), FROB (2014), and staff calculations.
Notes: FROB = Fondo de Reestructuración Ordenada Bancaria; SAREB = Sociedad de Gestión de Activos Procedentes de la Reestructuración Bancaria.

Figure 6.6 SAREB's Financial Structure

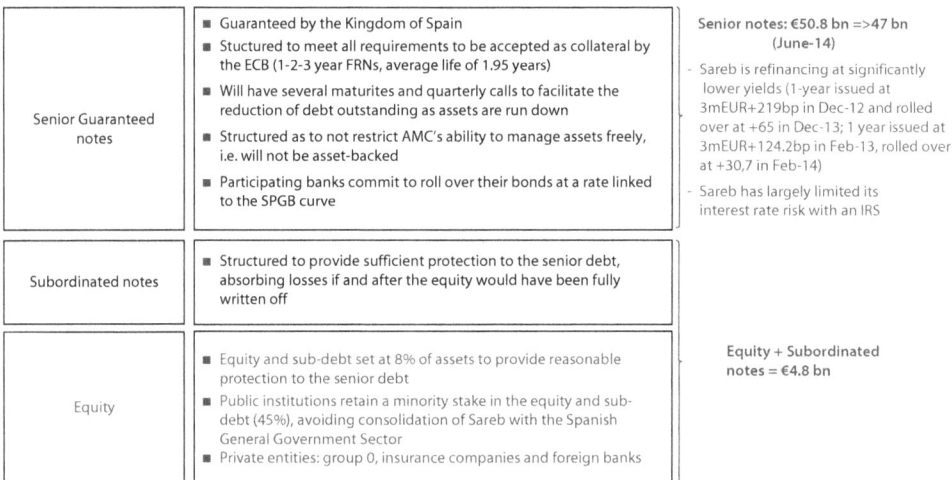

Source: FROB (2014).
Notes: FROB = Fondo de Reestructuración Ordenada Bancaria; SAREB = Sociedad de Gestión de Activos Procedentes de la Reestructuración Bancaria.

loans accounted for 78 percent of assets transferred by value but only 46 percent by number. The expeditious transfer was completed by December 2012 for group 1 and February 2013 for group 2.

Funding
SAREB's balance sheet was relatively highly leveraged, at approximately 11:1. To purchase assets, the company issued government-guaranteed senior notes (€50.8 billion), structured to meet requirements to be accepted as collateral by the European Central Bank. Equity (€1.2 billion) represented just 2.3 percent of senior debt, or 9.4 percent if subordinated debt (€3.6 billion) is included (figure 6.6). This

appears to be low, considering the use of the equity to pay the interest on the debt issued, provide for working capital, and absorb future impairments.

Performance and Initial Lessons Learned

It is difficult to assess SAREB's performance, given the short period of time it has been in existence. However, useful lessons learned during its operationalization phase are presented here.

An important challenge has been the use of an average discount rate to determine the transfer price. By its nature, an average price may result in above-average recovery rates for half of the portfolio, with a deep loss on the other half. The rapid initial transfer did not give SAREB time to check all the information on the assets. It was missing critical information on the loans such as the daily transactions on collections. Thus, it implemented an in-depth due diligence after the transfer and developed in-house models to value individual assets, many of which are held in SPVs. At the recommendation of the BoS, SAREB took extraordinary write-downs in 2013 and 2014 on subordinated loans and unsecured loans against debtors in insolvency (of about 2 percent of the initial transfer value of the portfolio).[21] Combined with losses on hedging derivatives, this consumed all of SAREB's equity (the 2014 annual report shows a negative equity equal to 3 percent of total assets).[22]

Servicing agreements with banks were not successful. SAREB initially entered into mandatory two-year servicing agreements with all the banks that transferred assets. However, the banks did not have the experience in asset management and were undergoing a severe internal restructuring process themselves. The fee structure did not provide sufficient incentives and was fraught with conflicts of interest (banks are keen to do business with customers and not to collect on behalf of SAREB). As a result, SAREB launched a competitive process to consolidate its servicing agreements. Four professional servicers were awarded five- to seven-year contracts [which include detailed key performance indicators (KPIs)] in 2014. The relatively lengthy time frame was explained by the need to let bidders recover their initial investment. In addition, the contract allows for a rollover for a further period of time to prevent inefficiencies at the end of the initial contract.

The organization matters for the efficiency of an AMC. SAREB updated its organization in May 2015 to address inefficiencies generated by the split in functions between loan transactions and real estate. A continuum of actions is required between loans and real estate assets: some loans may be recovered only through legal repossession, and the management of real estate assets needs to be supervised to ensure the debtors' commitments are honored. A single Business Directorate will oversee the functions of management of real estate, loans, and recoveries.

Although the situation of the banking sector has been improving, NPLs remain high. The liquidity and solvency positions of the sector have improved. As of March 2015, Spanish banks fully comply with the phased-in requirement of 60 percent for the liquidity coverage ratio. Banks have increased their nominal capital, mostly through reinvested earnings and equity issuance, and the Basel III CET1 capital ratio of the system has increased to an average of 11.8 percent, comfortably above the minimum regulatory levels. Provisions represented 57 percent of NPLs in March 2015. However, NPLs remain relatively high at 12.5 percent of total loans.

Notes

1. This covered all liabilities of Allied Irish Bank (AIB), Bank of Ireland, Anglo Irish Bank, Irish Life and Permanent, Irish Nationwide Building Society (INBS), and the Educational Building Society (EBS), representing 68 percent of all banking assets in the country. Certain banking subsidiaries of systemic importance in Ireland with a significant and broad presence in the domestic economy were eligible for the scheme.

2. Of the five credit institutions, one was nationalized, two had majority public ownership, and the other two would be either nationalized (INBS in August 2010) or restructured with state aid and merged with a larger public bank (EBS merged with AIB in August 2011).

3. When NAMA was set up in November 2009, the expected discount at the time was estimated at about 30 percent.

4. This applied to Bank of Ireland and Anglo Irish Bank. For the other participating banks, loans of less than €20 million were transferred.

5. NAMA acquired €74 billion of par debt, out of €158 billion in six property-based lending in the six Irish banks as of the end of 2008. However, NAMA did not acquire residential mortgages, or consumer and other loans (€270 billion).

6. Board members are nominated by either Central Bank of Nigeria (CBN), the Ministry of Finance, or Nigeria Deposit Insurance Corporation (NDIC); appointed by the president; and confirmed by the Senate. If a board member is incapacitated, the relevant entity nominates a replacement, and the same procedure is followed.

7. Addition of the various tranches, not actualized.

8. A 2012 audit shows asset impairment charges of ₦325 billion under local generally accepted accounting principles, and credit loss expense and fair value losses on investment property and financial assets of ₦238 billion under International Financial Reporting Standards (IFRS). Asset Management Corporation of Nigeria (AMCON) changed to IFRS accounting for the 2013 audit. See 2013 audited statements, p. 26.

9. AMCON's guidelines allow it to purchase any loan that poses a significant risk to an eligible institution, defined as reasonably expected to become substandard within three months or to result in a loss of at least 1 percent of assets within six months of the application to AMCON.

10. http://www.proshareng.com/news/15431.

11. Access Bank acquired Intercontinental Bank, Ecobank Transnational acquired Oceanic Bank, FCMB acquired FinBank, Sterling Bank acquired Equatorial Trust Bank, and African Capital Alliance acquired Union Bank. The legal difficulties in overriding shareholders' rights (a write-down of capital requires a shareholder vote) have played an important role in the transactions.

12. The 2011 audited accounts show an impairment charge of ₦1 trillion for four of these banks (Union Bank had not been sold at the date of the audit).

13. According to the 2014 Annual report (p. 40), the investments into Enterprise and Mainstreet were valued at ₦560 billion. Both investments were significantly impaired, and the cash consideration received was ₦182 million. Although the annual report shows a gain on disposal as a result of applying impairment before the transaction, the transactions have contributed to the growing negative equity position of AMCON.

14. The fund may be able to provide for debt repayment if banking system assets were to grow at 20 percent annually and AMCON incurred no further losses (based on banking sector assets of ₦27 trillion as of December 2014, and total CBN contributions capped at ₦500 billion). All financial institutions contributed to the fund in 2013.

15. Best practices in accordance with the Key Attributes for Effective Resolution Regimes, issued in October 2011, which states that losses should be allocated to shareholders and unsecured and uninsured creditors, to avoid exposing taxpayers to losses.

16. The new provisioning rules in 2012 led to an increase in the coverage of real estate developers' nonperforming loans (NPLs) from 17 to 43 percent.

17. Available at http://ec.europa.eu/economy_finance/eu_borrower/mou/spain-mou_en.pdf.

18. Sociedad de Gestión de Activos Procedentes de la Reestructuración Bancaria (SAREB) was 55 percent owned by private institutions, and 45 percent owned by the Fondo de Reestructuración Ordenada Bancaria (FROB).

19. Banco Financiero y de Ahorros—Bankia, S.A.; NCG Banco, S.A.; Catalunya Banc, S.A.; Banco de Valencia, S.A.; and Banco Gallego, S.A.

20. Banco Grupo Cajatres, S.A.; Banco Mare Nostrum, Banco de Caja España de Inversiones, Salamanca y Soria, S.A.; and Liberbank, S.A.

21. A forthcoming accounting regulation for SAREB from the BoS is expected to allow a compensation scheme in which only net losses will be registered in the profit and loss statement, netting out potential losses and potential gains (information as of August 2015).

22. Equity is affected, in 2013 as in 2014, by the effects of the interest rate hedge entered into in July 2013. SAREB's debt is at a floating rate, and assets do not generate returns linked to the interest rate (NPLs decrease over time). Some 80 percent of the debt is hedged with interest rate swaps to transform interest expenses into a fixed rate for nine years. The evolution of interest rates, down from the market rates in July 2013, has generated a negative valuation for the interest rate swaps, which has to be reflected against equity according to IFRS.

Bibliography

Aiyar, S., W. Bergthaler, J. Garrido, A. Ilyina, A. Jobst, K. Kang, D. Kovtun, Y. Liu, D. Monaghan, and M. Moretti. 2015. "A Strategy for Resolving Europe's Problem Loans." IMF Staff Discussion Note, SDN/15/19, International Monetary Fund, Washington, DC.

Claessens, S., C. Pazarbasioglu, L. Laeven, M. Dobler, F. Valencia, O. Nedelescu, and K. Seal. 2011. "Crisis Management and Resolution: Early Lessons from the Financial Crisis." IMF Staff Discussion Note, SDN 11/05, International Monetary Fund, Washington, DC.

Erbenova, M., Y. Liu, and M. Saxegaard. 2011. "Corporate and Household Debt Distress in Latvia: Strengthening the Incentives for a Market-Based Approach to Debt Resolution." IMF Working Paper, 11/85, International Monetary Fund, Washington, DC.

Fung, B., J. George, S. Hohl, and G. Ma. 2004. "Public Asset Management Companies in East Asia, A Comparative Study Together with Case Studies." Occasional Paper No. 3, Bank for International Settlements, Basel.

Ingves, S., S. Seelig, and D. He. 2004. "Issues in the Establishment of Asset Management Companies." IMF Policy Discussion Paper, Monetary and Financial Systems Department PDP/04/3, International Monetary Fund, Washington, DC.

Laeven, L., and T. Laryea. 2009. "Principles of Household Debt Restructuring." IMF Staff Position Note, SPN09/15, International Monetary Fund, Washington, DC.

Laryea, T. 2010. "Approaches to Corporate Debt Restructuring in the Wake of Financial Crisis." IMF Staff Position Note, SPN10/02, International Monetary Fund, Washington, DC.

Lindgren, C.-J., T. Balino, C. Enoch, A. Gulde, M. Quintyn, and L. Teo. 1999. "Financial Sector Crisis and Restructuring Lessons from Asia." IMF Occasional Paper 188, International Monetary Fund, Washington, DC.

Klingebiel, D. 2001. "The Use of Asset Management Companies in the Resolution of Banking Crises—Cross Country Experiences." World Bank, Washington, DC, http://www-wds.worldbank.org/servlet/WDSContentServer/WDSP/IB/2000/03/03/000094946_00021806025471/additional/128528322_20041117153059.pdf

Rose, T. 2001. "A Practical Guide to an Effective National AMC." World Bank Working Paper 32006, World Bank, Washington, DC, http://documents.worldbank.org/curated/en/2005/03/5721570/practical-guide-effective-national-amc.

Sanders, M. 2006. "Privately Managed Privatization in the Czech Republic." Jefferson Institute, Washington, DC, http://jeffersoninst.org/research/Economy/project/232.

Stone, M. R. 2002. "Corporate Sector Restructuring: The Role of Government in Times of Crisis." In *Economic Issues* 31, Washington, DC: International Monetary Fund.

Woo, D. 2000. "Two Approaches to Resolving Nonperforming Assets During Financial Crises." IMF Working Paper, WP/00/33, International Monetary Fund, Washington, DC.

Resolution Trust Corporation (RTC), United States

FDIC (Federal Deposit Insurance Corporation). 1997. *History of the Eighties: Lessons for the Future*, Volumes 1 & 2. Washington, DC: FDIC.

———. 1998. *Managing the Crisis: The FDIC and RTC Experience 1980–1994*, Volumes 1 & 2. Washington, DC: FDIC.

RTC OPRS (Resolution Trust Corporation, Office of Planning, Research, and Statistics). 1996. *Statistical Abstract, August 1989/September 1995*. Washington, DC: RTC.

All of the above may be found at https://www.fdic.gov.

Securum, Sweden

Bergström, C., P. Englund, and P. Thorell. 2003. "Securum and the Way Out of the Banking Crisis." Summary of a report commissioned by SNS (Centre for Business and Policy Studies), Stockholm.

Englund, P. 1999. "The Swedish Banking Crisis: Roots and Consequences." *Oxford Review of Economic Policy* 15 (3): 80–97.

Lybeck, J. A. 1993. *Finansiella Kriser Förr och Nu*. Stockholm: SNS Förlag.

Sandberg, Nils-Eric, R. Fagerfjäll, S. Lundström, K. Petterson, H. T. Söderström, and E. Åsbrink eds. 2005. *Vad Kan Vi Lära av Kraschen? Bank- och Fastighetskrisen, 1990–1993*. Stockholm: SNS Förlag.

Wallander, J. 1994. "Bankkrisen—Omfattning, Orsaker, Lärdomar [The Banking Crisis—Magnitude, Causes, Lessons]." In *Bankkrisen*, Stockholm: Bankkriskommittén.

Korea Asset Management Corporation (KAMCO), Korea

Balino, T. J., and A. Ubide. 1999. "The Korean Financial Crisis of 1997—A Strategy of Financial Sector Reform." IMF Working Paper No. 99/28, International Monetary Fund, Washington, DC.

Chopra, A., K. Kang, M. Karasulu, H. Liang, H. Ma, and A. Richards. 2002. "From Crisis to Recovery in Korea: Strategy, Achievements, and Lessons." IMF Working Paper No. 01/ 154, International Monetary Fund, Washington, DC.

He, Dong. 2004. "The Role of KAMCO in Resolving Nonperforming Loans in the Republic of Korea." IMF Working Paper No. 04/172, International Monetary Fund, Washington, DC.

Korea Asset Management Corporation. 2000. "Nov. 1997–Aug. 2000 KAMCO Experience: Non-Performing Asset Management and Resolution." KAMCO, Seoul.

———. 2003. "Korean Experience of Securitization and NPL Disposition." KAMCO, Seoul.

Lieberman, I., M. Gobbo, W. Mako, and R. Neyens. 2005. "Recent International Experiences in the Use of Voluntary Workouts under Distressed Conditions." In *Corporate Restructuring, Lessons from Experience*, edited by M. Pomerleano and W. Shaw, chapter 3, 59–98. World Bank: Washington, D.C.

Indonesian Bank Restructuring Agency (IBRA), Indonesia

Arnold, W. 2003. "Indonesian Bank Agency Fading Out." *New York Times*, October 2.

Barents Group of KPMG Consulting LLC. 2002. "IBRA Final Report."

Enoch, C., B. Baldwin, O. Frecaut, and A. Kovanen. 2001. "Indonesia: Anatomy of a Banking Crisis: Two Years of Living Dangerously—1997–99." IMF Working Paper 01/52, International Monetary Fund, Washington, DC.

IMF (International Monetary Fund). 2002. "Indonesian Country Report 02/154." IMF, Washington, DC.

———. 2004. "Indonesian Country Report 04/189." IMF, Washington, DC.

Lehman Brothers. 2000. "Indonesian Banks Revived, IBRA Reboots the System." Research report, New York.

Danaharta (Malaysia)

Athukorala, P. 2003. "FDI in Crisis and Recovery: Lessons from the 1997–98 Asian Crisis." *Australian Economic History Review* 43 (2): 197–213.

Bank Negara Malaysia. 2000. "Danamodal Nasional Berhad—the Malaysian Approach to Bank Recapitalisation, Revitalisation and Restructuring."

Danaharta. 2005. "Final Report."

Government of Indonesia. 1998. Pengurusan Danaharta Nasional Berhad Act.

Nambiar, S. 2009. "Malaysia and the Global Crisis: Impact, Response and Rebalancing Strategy." ADBI Working Paper 148, Asian Development Bank Institute, Manila.

Schiffrin, A. "Capital Controls: Malaysia." Initiative for policy dialogue, http://policydialogue.org/publications/backgrounders/casestudies/capital_controls_malaysia/en/.

Savings Deposit Insurance Fund (SDIF), Turkey

Akdağ, C. 2011a. "Managing Assets: Asset Valuation Process of SDIF." http://www.finrep.kiev.ua/download/12_dgf_15feb11_en.pdf.

———. 2011b. "Managing Assets: SDIF's Experience," http://www.finrep.kiev.ua/download/6_7_dgf_15feb11_en.pdf

Akyuz, Y. I., and K. Boratov. 2002. The Making of the Turkish Financial Crisis, United Nations Conference on Trade and Development, Geneva, Switzerland.

BRSA (Bank Regulation and Supervision Agency). 2003. "Banking Sector Restructuring Program Progress Report—(VII)." BRSA, Ankara.

———. 2012. "From Crisis to Financial Stability (Turkey Experience)." Working Paper (Revised Third Edition), BRSA, Ankara.

Rabo Bank. 2013. "The Turkish 2000–01 Banking Crisis." Economic Research Report, https://economics.rabobank.com/publications/2013/september/the-turkish-2000-01-banking-crisis.

SDIF (Savings Deposit Insurance Fund). 2002–2007. Annual Reports. http://www.tmsf.org.tr/yillik.rapor.en.

———. 2011. "Bank Resolution Experience." http://www.finrep.kiev.ua/download/5_dgf_15feb11_en.pdf.

———. 2013. "Bank Resolution Experience of the SDIF." http://www.raftemizligi.com/Content/E-Kitaplar.ph.

World Bank. 2000. "Proposed Financial Sector Adjustment Loan." Report No. P 7356 TU, November, http://documents.worldbank.org/curated/en/2000/11/735352/turkey-financial-sector-adjustment-loan-project.

———. 2001. "Turkey—Programmatic Financial and Public Sector Adjustment Loan Project." ReportNo.7463TU,June,http://documents.worldbank.org/curated/en/2001/06/1346425/turkey-programmatic-financial-public-sector-adjustment-loan-project.

———. 2010. "An Assessment of the Corporate Restructuring Framework Background Note." World Bank, Washington, DC.

National Asset Management Agency (NAMA), Ireland

Bacon P. 2009. "Evaluation of Options for Resolving Property Loan Impairments and Associated Capital Adequacy of Irish Credit Institutions: Proposal for a National Asset Management Agency (NAMA)." National Treasury Management Agency, Dublin.

Commission of Investigation. 2011. "Misjudging Risk: Causes of the Systemic Banking Crisis in Ireland: Report of the Commission of Investigation into the Banking Sector in Ireland."

Deegan, G., 2015, "High-Flyers Quit Nama with €42,000 Payoff," *The Times of London*, October 10.

European Commission. 2009. State Aid N 349/2009—Ireland, Credit Institutions Eligible Liabilities Guarantee Scheme.

———. 2010. State Aid 725/2009—Ireland, Establishment of a National Asset Management Company: Asset Relief Scheme for Banks in Ireland.

Honohan, P. 2009. "Resolving Ireland's Banking Crisis." *The Economic and Social Review* 40 (2): 207–31.

———. 2010. "The Irish Banking Crisis and Regulatory and Financial Stability Policy, 2003–2008." A Report to the Minister for Finance by the Governor of the Central Bank, Dublin.

———. 2012. "Recapitalisation of Failed Banks—Some Lessons from the Irish Experience." Address at the 44th Annual Money, Macro and Finance Conference, Trinity College, Dublin.

NAMA. Key Financial Figures. https://www.nama.ie/financial/key-financial-figures/.

NAMA Comptroller and Auditor General. 2010. "Special Report 76 (2010), National Asset Management Agency– Acquisition of Bank Assets."

———. 2014. "Special Report (2014) NAMA: Progress Report 2010–2012."

Shoenmaker, D. 2015. "Stabilizing and Healing the Irish Banking System, Policy Lessons." Paper prepared for the CBI-CEPR-IMF Conference—Lessons from its Recovery from the Bank-Sovereign Loop, Ireland.

Asset Management Corporation of Nigeria (AMCON), Nigeria

Alford, D. E. 2012. "Reform of the Nigerian Banking System—Assessment of the Asset Management Corporation of Nigeria (AMCON) and Recent Developments."

———. 2010. Guidelines. http://amcon.com.ng/documents/AMCON-Guidelines.aspx.

———. 2013, 2014. Annual reports. AMCON.

———. 2014. "Loans Purchased from Various Eligible Financial Institutions (EFIs)." http://www.amcon.com.ng/About-our-work.aspx.

Central Bank of Nigeria. 2014. "Financial Stability Report."

Financial Stability Board. 2011. "Key Attributes for Effective Resolution Regimes."

Ighomwenghian, K. 2011. "Another Look at Purchase of Zenon, Others' N275b Loans by AMCON." http://www.proshareng.com/news/15431.

International Monetary Fund. 2015. "Nigeria 2014 Article IV." International Monetary Fund, Washington, DC.

Makanjuola, Y. 2015. *Banking Reform in Nigeria: The Aftermath of the 2009 Financial Crisis.* New York: McMillan.

Nationwide. 2014. "AMCON Turns Distressed Bank—Loses N2.44 Trillion in 3 Years!" http://www.nationwidenews.net/?p=4150.

Philipps, S., and A. James. 2014. "A Special Report on the Nigerian Banking System: The Ripple Effects of Lehman—A Tale of Sin and Redemption?"

World Bank. 2007. "Report on Observance of Standards and Codes: Nigeria, Insolvency, and Creditor Rights." World Bank, Washington, DC.

World Bank, International Monetary Fund. 2013. "Nigeria Financial Sector Assessment Program. 2013: Crisis Management and Crisis Preparedness Frameworks" Technical Note. http://www-wds.worldbank.org/external/default/WDSContentServer/WDSP/IB/2013/09/02/000442464_20130902142935/Rendered/PDF/807330ESW0Nige00 Box379814B00Public0.pdf

Sociedad de Gestión de Activos Procedentes de la Reestructuración Bancaria (SAREB), Spain

European Commission. 2012. Memorandum of Understanding between the European Commission and Spain, Brussels, July 20, http://ec.europa.eu/economy_finance/eu_borrower/mou/spain-mou_en.pdf.

European Commission, Directorate-General for Economic and Financial Affairs. 2014. "Spain—Post Programme Surveillance—Spring 2014 Report." European Economy Occasional Papers 193, http://ec.europa.eu/economy_finance/publications/occasional_paper/2014/pdf/ocp193_en.pdf.

FROB (Fondo de Reestructuración Ordenada Bancaria). 2014. Investor presentations, http://www.frob.es/es/Documents/20141223Presentación%20FROB%20prot.pdf.

Government of Spain. Ley 9/2012, de reestructuración y resolución de entidades de crédito. (Disposición Adicional Novena).

International Monetary Fund. 2012. "Spain: Financial Sector Stability Assessment."

———. 2014. "Spain: Financial Sector Reforms, Final Progress Report."

———. 2015. Spain, Article IV.

Ortega, E., and J. Peñalosa. 2012. "The Spanish Economic Crisis: Key Factors and Growth Challenges in the Euro Area." Documentos Ocasionales No. 1201, Bank of Spain.

Sociedad de Gestión de Activos Procedentes de la Reestructuración Bancaria. 2013, 2014. Annual Report.

ECO-AUDIT

Environmental Benefits Statement

The World Bank Group is committed to reducing its environmental footprint. In support of this commitment, the Publishing and Knowledge Division leverages electronic publishing options and print-on-demand technology, which is located in regional hubs worldwide. Together, these initiatives enable print runs to be lowered and shipping distances decreased, resulting in reduced paper consumption, chemical use, greenhouse gas emissions, and waste.

The Publishing and Knowledge Division follows the recommended standards for paper use set by the Green Press Initiative. The majority of our books are printed on Forest Stewardship Council (FSC)–certified paper, with nearly all containing 50–100 percent recycled content. The recycled fiber in our book paper is either unbleached or bleached using totally chlorine free (TCF), processed chlorine free (PCF), or enhanced elemental chlorine free (EECF) processes.

More information about the Bank's environmental philosophy can be found at http://www.worldbank.org/corporateresponsibility.

green press
INITIATIVE

www.ingramcontent.com/pod-product-compliance
Lightning Source LLC
Chambersburg PA
CBHW080556220326
41599CB00032B/6496